Flylines & Fishtales

Flylines & Fishtales

THE STORY OF GLIMPSE LAKE LODGE

John Grain

CAITLIN PRESS

Caitlin Press
Distributed by Harbour Publishing
PO Box 219
Madeira Park, BC, Canada V0N 2H0
www.caitlin-press.com

Printed and bound in Canada

Library and Archives Canada Cataloguing in Publication

Grain, John, 1950–
       Flylines and fishtales : the story of Glimpse Lake Lodge / John Grain.

ISBN 978-1-894759-26-7

       1. Grain, John, 1950–. 2. Glimpse Lake Lodge—History.
3. Fishing lodges—British Columbia—Merritt Region—History.
4. Merritt Region (B.C.)—Biography. I. Title.
SH572.B8G73 2007   971.1'72   C2007-907363-8

To Kirsti, my wife, my bride and my best friend who has always loved, trusted, supported and encouraged me.
You have kept me focused and without you I would be lost.

and also

To our children, Kristoffer, John-Erik and Kari. For all the time you spent at the camp, we can only offer you the memories of a magical time and a magical place.
We hope they will always be as fond as ours.
This book is the closest I can come to passing on to you that "little piece of paradise separated from the rest of the world by four thousand feet and a few gates."

Contents

Preface

Just north of Merritt, British Columbia, lies the Nicola Plateau. It is an undulating plain over thirteen hundred metres in elevation that separates the Nicola and Okanagan Valleys. Its wealth of forests and vast expanses of grassland punctuated with countless lakes and streams make it ideal for fishing, hiking and hunting. Thirteen kilometres north of Salmon Lake Road, which bisects the plateau, lies a tiny, picturesque gem: Glimpse Lake. At the far end are the remnants of an early homestead; a cluster of buildings with an intriguing history.

Most of the property bordering the lake was originally a fox farm, which closed in the late thirties when it became unprofitable. It was replaced by Glimpse Lake fishing camp, which was established by a Swiss immigrant, Bob Albrecht, and his wife Helen. They operated it for thirty years but in the late 1960s, the land was sold to a developer from Kamloops. He kept the camp, along with the 160-acre parcel on which it was located intact, and leased it out as a business. The rest of the water frontage and much of the surrounding area was subdivided and sold to private interests. Today, a variety of structures from simple one-room cabins to sprawling summer homes rim the south end of the lake.

In 1981 Terra-7 Investments, a group of investors of which I was part, purchased the fishing camp property and named it "Glimpse

Lake Lodge." We sold it in 1987 to a European concern representing the Relais/Chateaux Hotel chain, who suspended the fishing camp operation.

This book provides a brief history of the fishing camp and the original homesteaders, Bob and Helen Albrecht. It also relates some of the hilarious, heartbreaking, tender and often absurd episodes that we experienced during our years of ownership. There were also seven other partners, each of whom, I am certain, could fill a volume with their own adventures and contributions.

The success of Glimpse Lake Lodge during our "era" is the direct result of not only the partners, but more importantly, their spouses, enthusiastic families and scores of willing and eager friends. For any oversights, omissions or lapses in memory, I apologize to my partners and ask for their understanding.

John Grain
Kelowna, BC

Foreword

*O*wning a fishing camp is an elusive dream for many, as it was for me until 1981 when we purchased Glimpse Lake Lodge. It was a monumental risk, but in retrospect, worth every penny, every sacrifice and every ounce of effort. For my wife and I, the experience created the blueprint for a happy and fulfilling life.

Operating the camp was truly a formative time for a young family. This was where our children learned about nature, beauty, the environment and hard work and where I learned about dedication, loyalty, trust and compromise. This was also where I learned about co-operation, sharing and integrity. Most importantly, I learned these things with my wife Kirsti at my side. This was the "stuff of life," cementing a relationship that has produced three wonderful children, a love and a life that I am honoured to share.

It was only after we sold the property that I realized the value of this amazing six-year adventure. Not only did it develop wisdom and understanding, it moulded our values, morals and character. Life's truest rewards, I have discovered in the sixteen years since I first penned the outline for this book, are most often found in the simplest experiences. Our time at Glimpse Lake was an endless series of such little lessons. I felt compelled to preserve and share some of them before the fading memory of old age either obliterated them totally or exaggerated them beyond belief. *Flylines and Fishtales* is an attempt to do that. It is also an attempt to recognize and therefore honour the time, love and hard work of the pioneers who forged this fascinating chapter of BC history.

1

A Long and Winding Road

"Whispering," my father used to say, "is the best way to get someone's attention." The hushed conversation across the lunchroom table between two co-workers certainly had captured mine. Through the secretive dialogue I heard snippets of "huge fish" and "a beautiful lake." My interest had been piqued and after a series of discreet inquiries, I underlined Glimpse Lake on a map of southern British Columbia. Leaving my summer job with Air Canada at the Vancouver International Airport, and determined to squeeze in a fishing trip before starting my final year at the University of British Columbia, I made plans for the day-long drive to the interior of the province. Also, I had promised my wife Kirsti a romantic weekend away before the birth of our first child, which was only weeks away.

Buoyed with the self-confidence of youth, I fancied myself a seasoned fly-fisherman, having started a course in fly-tying the previous month. Not wanting to shatter the dream, I was determined to find a lake containing at least one fish, perhaps genetically challenged or otherwise sufficiently addled to mistake my homemade offering for something resembling its natural diet.

Equipped with a collection of unidentifiable flies, the results of my first efforts at tying, Kirsti and I left Vancouver early one Saturday morning in the early summer of 1975. Our destination was the sleepy southern interior town of Merritt, BC, and hopefully, one of the many lakes on the surrounding Nicola Plateau. Lacking specific directions, I wisely equipped myself with a map, printed on a place-mat from a Merritt restaurant where we had stopped after the gruelling drive through the Fraser Canyon. The slogan across the top of the mat boasted "A Lake a Day as Long as You Stay!"—an enticement that made me shudder with anticipation. In the bottom right-hand corner, partially obliterated by the soup I had spilled in my haste to get moving and catch the big one, was a mileage chart. It claimed that Glimpse Lake, a fishing camp, was a mere forty-minute drive away along an all-season road.

Because I was unwilling to tarnish my male ego by asking directions at the Tourist Information booth, this short drive became a four-hour marathon. Armed with assurances of success, a questionable sense of direction, and a full tank of gas, we boldly ventured north along Highway 5 into the high country of the Nicola Plateau. We were totally unaware that we had set in motion a series of events that would alter our destinies.

The gravel road began as soon as we left the main highway at the turnoff leading to Peterhope Lake. Our trusty Toyota valiantly scraped through cavernous potholes and over decrepit bridges until we lurched to a halt surrounded by a herd of cattle. They were convinced that our car made an ideal scratching post! For what seemed like hours we sweltered motionless in the afternoon heat, choking on the stink, the dust and the flies. We were only able to escape when an aged truck of questionable lineage arrived from the opposite direction and simply nudged its way through the stubborn throng. We quickly did the same and soon after arrived at a BC Forest Service camp idyllically situated in a grassy meadow on the shores of Peterhope Lake. Toasting our good fortune at being the sole occupants of the camp, we decided to make a picnic lunch and unpacked our icebox. Moments later, our high spirits were shattered.

"John!" Kirsti screamed.

I looked up to see a large black bear and two cubs materialize as if by magic from the nearby forest. Then they ambled curiously towards us! Dropping our food-laden paper plates, we dashed to the relative safety of the car, almost tripping over each other in the process. We stared in amazement from inside as the bears methodically inspected and devoured most of our supplies. They were oblivious to the grating, mechanical sounds of the vehicle, the blaring horn and our own hysterical shrieks and gestures. Finally the bears had their fill and wandered back into the trees. We snatched up what was left of our picnic, and raced away, still hungry but happy to be safe.

Again we consulted our trusty restaurant map and drove on, certain that the elusive Glimpse Lake was just around the next corner. For the next few hours we inspected swamps, logging landings, garbage dumps and a myriad of other dead-ends. Clearly we were lost. The rough roads and the occasional groan from Kirsti reminded me that a premature labour would be a really bad situation. I was becoming more and more uneasy about being so far from a hospital. Ultimately, we detected the glint of a body of water through the distant trees, hence the name Glimpse Lake I supposed, and eagerly wound our way towards it.

A peeling sign claimed it was Glimpse Lake as I had hoped. In the gathering dusk, a knowing eye would have detected rings in the mirror-like surface as abundant as droplets from a spring shower. A seasoned fisherman would have seen the cloudless sky and realized that the cause was not rain, but rising fish!

The private summer cabins along the lakeshore were empty and seemed threatening. In the growing darkness, there was no sign of a fishing camp. The only road seemed little more than a cart trail, and meandered through an encroaching forest along the north shore of the lake. Losing the battle to the depression that often accompanies fatigue, I decided to follow the "road," though nearly overcome with the fear and panic of isolation. After only a few hundred metres, I was willing to admit defeat and was about to turn around and try to retrace our path back to civilization. Unexpectedly, a gleam of light shot through the gloom ahead. The trees thinned, and we inched past a flagging snake fence and the ghostly image of what appeared to be an aged barn on the verge of collapse. Ahead, the dim flickering of storm lanterns promised habitation.

Through the swirling veils of woodsmoke, a two-level log home emerged, complete with a weathered and rusted corrugated iron roof and a dangerous-looking veranda. The geraniums and petunias, strangely out of place, beckoned to us from unpainted window boxes. With typical urban suspicion, we abandoned the safety of the car and approached an uneven, rough-sawn porch. Nailed to the door was a crude plywood sign. The hand-written scrawl welcomed us to Glimpse Lake and directed us to "knock loud" upon arrival.

Following the instructions, we were soon rewarded by the clamour of human footfalls from inside. Moments later, the door burst open amid the clatter of a small cowbell hung over the threshold and designed, we assumed, to let the owners know when a customer came in. A stocky, balding man greeted us. He was wearing a pair of well-worn, ample jeans that bore the scars of many amateurish attempts at darning. The red suspenders, with the faded letters STIHL, had been hastily secured over a whitish T-shirt. With a broad, friendly smile, he invited us into the cozy office, where he lit another lantern and introduced himself.

Our host, Bruce Grant, operated the fishing camp with his wife Belle. They had done so since about 1970, leasing the business from an absentee owner. The lines of fatigue on their faces were silent reminders of the rigours of daily life in the camp. He was a wiry, middle-aged man who seemed dismayed by the two misplaced city folk standing expectantly in front of him. A grey stubble of a beard, scarred and callused hands and hundreds of tiny flecks of paint on his face betrayed the fact that the hours of the day had again run out before he had reached the end of his job list. Belle simply looked tired and as we correctly thought, her health was not good.

Sipping a half-cup of coffee poured from a pot simmering on the huge wood stove, we were disappointed to learn that all the cabins had been booked. But, with the country hospitality that would soon become very familiar, Bruce said that no one had ever been turned away after driving so far. Clearly, casting a wary eye at Kirsti's bulging stomach, he was not about to change his policy now. Instead, he suggested that we could take the one cabin that was still vacant. Although it had been booked, the guests hadn't arrived yet. He reasoned that because it was already so late, the people probably wouldn't get there that night. If they did, the couch in the lodge would have to be good enough! So while Bruce bustled to gather paper, dry kindling, a water bucket and a lantern, I made an initial inspection of the surroundings.

The interior of the lodge was heavy with age and deterioration. Every cranny seemed to promise a secret or faded memory. Its rugged, hand-hewn log walls were sparsely chinked with a mixture of newspaper, moss, sawdust, mud and a foreign material that reminded me of barn-yard waste. The many gaps and draughts bore silent testimony to years of good intentions fallen victim to procrastination. A simple, hardwood floor strewn with clashing fragments of carpet and sticks of antique furniture surrounded a central barrel-stove carelessly stuffed into the yawning mouth of the fireplace. An upright piano peeked from the farthest corner of the living room. A fox pelt, rusted traps and peeling pictures were scattered randomly on walls and straining beams. The head of a deer hung motionless, nailed to an open space between the windows. Dusty, glass orbs stared vacantly from a tattered attempt at taxidermy. It spoke of a time when the gifts of nature were much more abundant.

The business end of the operation was tucked into a small niche near the front door. Its two pine tables were strewn with papers and a dog-eared reservation book occupied an influential place in the centre. The radio-phone, its brackets bolted to the table, crackled incoherently, creating the momentary illusion of companionship. The smell of woodsmoke and the aroma of dinner still lingered, reminding us that the bears had stolen our lunch and we hadn't eaten since.

Bruce's return interrupted my thoughts and, brushing away my weak apologies for arriving so late, he led us to a tiny, one-room cabin on the lakeshore. In later years I would hear a guest, a fellow with a strong southern accent, exclaim to his wife, "My dear, this cabin ain't rustic—it's positively SPARTAN! We'll take it!"

With a combination of relief and concern, we moved in while Bruce lit the lantern and brought two buckets of drinking water. My quizzical gaze at the oven prompted Bruce to give us a brief sermon on the structure and workings of a wood-burning stove. Finally he wished us good-night and limped out the door.

We put in a good supply of kindling and logs for the night and, after a snack, took a closer look at the very basic but functional cabin. Messages carved into logs boasted of prior fishing success and guaranteed a "good time" if we wanted to phone a certain local number. The walls, though solid, were draughty due to missing sections of chinking that had fallen or been pried out of the spaces between the logs. The purpose of the tin cans hanging from exposed rafters puzzled us. As we discovered during the first heavy rain, they were strategically located to catch the drips from leaks in the roof in the event that necessary repairs had not been completed in time! We were equally puzzled by the naked, inert forty-watt light bulb dangling from an atrophied filament of copper wire. There was no switch to turn it on or off! Linoleum, curled at the edges and pock-marked with burns from cinders or careless smokers, was nailed to the floor with roofing tacks. The single window, a broken corner of one pane stuffed with tissue paper, rattled eerily in the inky darkness.

Fatigue eventually overcame our curiosity. We eagerly went to bed for the night, promptly rolling into the centre of a huge, sagging mattress, wondering about what the following day might hold. After we blew out the lantern, the sound of scurrying and scampering in the walls revealed the disturbing presence of mice or various other varmints. Kirsti buried her head under the quilt and voluminous pillows, convinced that the mice would nibble on her unprotected eyelids once she fell asleep. Finally, we drifted off into a delicious slumber. My final vague recollection of that memorable evening was the disconcerting visibility of stars through the presumably protective roof!

Living in the city, one either ignores or becomes accustomed to the many sounds that invade our daily lives. It was the silence early the next morning that woke us. Stepping out to the fragile porch, I strained to detect even the faintest whisper of activity, only to be drowned out by the thump of my own heart. I could almost hear the tiny spider, slogging as if drugged, between the dew-drenched threads of its web, which hung between the weathered steps. The trance was burst by an arrogant squirrel that shattered the silence with his impatient chatter.

Imperceptibly, the black and white starkness of pre-dawn softened. In the first breath of morning the infant aspen leaves chuckled approvingly. The surface of the lake burst forth and its silken mirror shattered into a thousand diamonds. The emerging sun cast welcoming rays over the treetops. The morning mists spiralled upwards and disintegrated like an imaginary veil. The lake was perfect; proud, unencumbered and pure.

Gradually the community came to life and the cries of resident loons, blackbirds and terns became a chorus, interspersed with the splash of rising fish and the remote murmur of cattle. The fragrance of grass, hay, wild flowers and the forest enhanced the serenity and created a heady perfume. Like the victims of mythical sirens, Kirsti and I had fallen under the spell of Nature's miracle. We had discovered a paradise and already, Glimpse Lake felt more like home than home did! We vowed to return as often as we could, which we did for the next three years whenever the opportunity presented itself.

2

The Last Straw

here were no sirens. With monotonous regularity, the flashing police lights danced from blue to red to white off the bedroom walls, magnified grotesquely by the full-length mirror of our dresser. Five years of university had given me a wonderful education but never prepared me for this. How I hated the street lights, the noise of the traffic and the stink of exhaust.

The previous week's break-in at the 7-11 next door had upset us enough, and now there was this. Our elderly neighbour, while walking his dog, had found the body just before dusk. The lot was kitty-corner across the street from our bungalow in White Rock, an upscale suburb of Vancouver, BC. The crumbling cement foundation was a stark reminder of the house that had burned to the ground two years earlier. Two blackened cedars flanked the cracked sidewalk. A flight of three concrete stairs led to a gaping cavern that was once a basement. Because the body couldn't be seen from the road, I guessed it had been there for a while, probably dumped some time the night before. What a great place to raise my family!

The notion of bringing up three-year-old Kristoffer and newly born John-Erik in an unsavoury suburban environment revolted us. Jobs, house, kids and a car. Our commitments, it seemed, had trapped us. We weren't city people and we yearned for a slower, uncomplicated life. We longed for a clean, quiet place to live where children could be raised in safety surrounded by trees, not buildings. Yet it was in the city, with violence and crime our constant companions, that it seemed we were destined to eke out our existence. Had we made the wrong decisions?

We just wanted to be back at the small, rundown fishing camp at Glimpse where we could relax, unwind and savour the simple pleasures of the outdoors. Our too-infrequent trips were about the only things that made the frustration and monotony in our lives bearable. We were unhappy and, clearly, something had to change. It was time to get serious about finding an alternative lifestyle for it seemed the dream of leaving the Lower Mainland was becoming more and more remote with each passing day.

It was pure economics. I was a teacher and Kirsti was a nurse. We both had permanent jobs. The sooner we moved, the cheaper we would be. As we both gained experience and seniority, the availability of jobs in education and health care diminished, as did our opportunities to relocate. As our experience increased, our services became more expensive for employers who wanted the biggest bang for their bucks.

The previous year, I had tried unsuccessfully for months to find a job outside of the Lower Mainland. Compounding the problem, by the late seventies, housing prices were beginning to rise uncontrollably in the urban areas. Believing that the ballooning residential market would expand to the interior, we had thought about buying some property, both as a hedge against soaring prices and as a recreational retreat and investment. Naturally, any Glimpse Lake real estate became our main interest. All we needed was money and a bit of luck.

3

Quirks of Fate

Dotting the south end of Glimpse Lake were a number of lakeshore lots, some of which had remained unsold since the initial creation of the subdivision years earlier. They were half an acre in size and were actually deeded property as opposed to the government leases which are so common in the BC wilderness areas. They had sat untended and seemingly forgotten for years and we had decided the timing was right to buy one. Uncertain as to whether or not our financial situation would even support such a move, we made a tentative offer by telephone on the only wooded one left, lot 20. We reasoned it would be pointless having property at Glimpse if it did not have lake frontage and trees. The subdivision also included a number of tier two and three lots set back from the lakeshore. Some of them had a view of the lake and were much larger, being around two and a half to five acres.

We waited anxiously to hear from the realtor and when the news came it was bad. Unbelievably, the lot we had bid on had sold! Someone else had bought it a few days earlier in the first real estate transaction on Glimpse in years! We were devastated, convinced the fates were against us.

Due to poor timing we had lost out, and once again our dreams seemed beyond reach. Strangely, it didn't even cross our minds to make an offer on the un-treed lots. Looking back now, it's hard to imagine being so short-sighted! With a combination of anger, resentment and remorse, we again reserved a cabin at the fishing camp for our Thanksgiving weekend outing in 1980.

On Thanksgiving Monday, the final day of the weekend, a seemingly insignificant event occurred as we were enjoying a walk with our infant sons. On that frosty morning, the fall colours a frenzy of yellow and gold, I noticed a strange figure in the distance. A man, conspicuous in his business suit and carrying an expensive engraved leather briefcase, had come out of the forest. He was engrossed in taking measurements with a well-worn tape measure.

My curiosity getting the better of me, I approached him.

"G'morning," I declared amicably. "That's the most expensive-looking fly-box I've ever seen!"

He laughed and held the briefcase up in his hands defensively stating, "I'm no fisherman . . . just a real estate appraiser. They want to sell this place and asked me to try to put a price on it."

"Well, what a coincidence. I'm looking for a fishing camp," I joked. "What's it worth?"

"They've got 160 acres of land but not much else here. The buildings are shot and the business is all but non-existent. It's really just a glorified cow pasture," he replied apathetically. "All I can do is make sure the survey map is right and try to figure out an asking price for the owner. He'll be lucky to get $250,000 for it," he continued.

"Who owns it?" I asked.

"A guy from Kamloops. He owns North Arm Aggregates and a bunch of other stuff there."

I thanked him and anxiously jogged back to where Kirsti and the kids were playing, equipped with my new-found knowledge. The cursory information about the pending sale of Glimpse Lake Lodge and the surrounding 160 acres intrigued me. Included in the purchase price of only $250,000 were the land, the business and all the assets including the boats, cabins and their contents. To me, it seemed a bargain.

The idea of becoming a fishing camp owner began to germinate, rekindling a wistful dream. Earlier, given that our attempt to buy a lot on the lake had fallen through, we wondered if this could be our second chance. Like excited children at Christmas, Kirsti and I drove back to Vancouver, our heads spinning at the possibilities.

With the realism that accompanies rational thought, the next morning brought doubt and scepticism. After all, the kids needed schools and friends, Kirsti and I were both working full-time and our only asset was our home. How could we live up to our commitments and responsibilities and even entertain the notion of trying to own and run a fishing camp as well? We were broke and the reality of our personal financial situation added to the growing list of barriers. We could simply not afford the $250,000 they were asking. Even if we could, there were too many other aspects of our lives that would have to be abandoned or changed to make it work.

I casually mentioned the pending sale of the Glimpse Lake property to my good friend and fellow teacher, Jack Dicken, who had once proposed the idea of forming an investment club. We decided to take another look at the idea and talked to some staff members who might be interested.

I was more than a little surprised at the end of the week to find that we had seven very interested individuals, even though most of them had never seen the property. In addition to myself, there were my fellow teachers Jack, Jo-Anne Beer, Evelyn Shadforth, Dorothy Nuthall, Gloria Ewan and Gloria's husband, Bruce Coleman. My parents, Peter and Hilda Grain, had recently retired and had offered to help operate the camp. When we asked to take them on as partners, they agreed. Terra-7 Investments was born!

By Christmas, we had negotiated an interim agreement for sale. As in most real estate deals, the sale was conditional upon us finding acceptable financing and inspecting of the assets and property itself. The vendor had agreed to carry the outstanding balance for a year so we did not see that aspect of the agreement to be problematic. However, most of the "assets" were still under winter's grip, making inspection almost impossible. But inspect we must and so we made tentative plans to view the property as soon as the weather permitted us to travel safely.

We waited that January for the Vancouver rains and snow to

abate and for the Arctic front to retreat past Kamloops, anxious to remove the subject clauses and finalize the purchase of our investment property. The days dragged on until one weekend in early February dawned clear, but still cold. However, enthusiasm overcame caution and we gathered the partners and spouses together. The trek, with its convoy of vehicles, began. We had phoned and told the sales agent in Kamloops about our plans. He assured us that the caretaker would be notified and he would be pleased to provide us with a guided tour as soon as we arrived.

How the winter in British Columbia's interior high country can transform a landscape! We were totally unprepared for what we found. The lake itself was under a foot of ice and the lakeshore and road were indistinguishable under mountainous drifts of snow. The last mile into the lodge was impassable and the lead car quickly became stuck in the smothering powder. We hadn't gone this far just to be denied by a few inches of snow, so we strapped on our cross-country skis for the final assault. We must have been a very strange sight. Clad in our best Vancouver winter-wear, we wormed our way toward the snow-bound homestead with which we would soon be intimately familiar. The airborne ice crystals sandblasting our ears heightened the sense of urgency and in short order we found ourselves gingerly rapping on the front door.

The smoking chimney signalled the presence of the caretaker, and we were dismayed to discover that we had wakened him. He was still sleeping at one in the afternoon! Our shock was complete when we were invited, through the back door, into the kitchen. The stench of marijuana was overpowering and the moist heat belching from the stove hit us like a blast furnace. Our surprise, however, was nothing compared to that of the poor caretaker. No one had told him that twelve strangers expected to view the entire camp, the assets and the property lines, and it was his task to show them! Somehow the message had not been delivered and he didn't seem too eager to help!

The winter had been especially harsh, being windier and colder than normal that year. The inefficient wood-burning stove in the large main lodge had not been able to maintain a comfortable temperature due to the poor insulation. As a result, the unfortunate caretaker had been driven into the kitchen for warmth. Dirty yellow batts of insulation hung from the uppermost part of the wall and were stuffed into the spaces between some of the logs in an attempt to keep in some of the heat. Ice from condensation caked the windows and soot-laden cobwebs drooped from the rafters.

The living room was filled with rowboats stacked three high and cluttered with garbage cans, buckets and various other equipment necessary for the operation of a fishing camp. It was, we were to discover, the only building that possessed any semblance of security. Specifically, the windows were sealed shut with rough timbers bolted through the log walls. In addition, four huge nails anchored the door in place. Finally there was a locking secret entrance through the bathroom window, though because we never found the key, it was never locked!

Bleary-eyed, the caretaker invited us to share the warmth of the country kitchen, though there was standing room only. Clearly, a single male occupied this dingy space. The availability of hot water and laundry facilities appeared to be limited, as we correctly concluded from the stacks of crusted dishes, faded floor and stained clothing hanging from nails driven at odd angles into the whitewashed walls. Our host was not a skilled domestic.

All we could think about was getting warm again, so we helped clear a path through the garbage, huddled around the stove and found some cups without mould. We poured hot water into them from a black kettle, caked on the inside with mineral deposits. In a few minutes we had prepared a brackish, steaming drink resembling instant coffee, which we gulped down thirstily.

After warming up, we made our first stab at matching the existing assets with the master list provided by the vendor. We soon recognized the futility in the task. The "fish preservation facility" described on the master list turned out to be a saw-dust shed that needed ice to be cut from the lake and stored during the winter! The worn and dented radio telephone was itemized as "the latest in modern communications technology." The "ample electricity supplied to every cabin from a modern generating plant" required the operator to start a single cylinder diesel engine with a hand-crank and hope that the rotting insulation drooping from the wires would not cause a short-circuit and torch the place or blow it to bits. The "modern refrigeration and cooking facilities" turned out to be a kerosene fridge, which was very efficient the one time we got it to work, and a huge wood stove built by the Adams Company in Toronto in 1906. The "fleet of rental boats" consisted of a few, hand-built clinker rowboats that actually floated and had oars and oarlocks, though they were in a terrible state of disrepair. There were also six or seven other boats, most of which would eventually be better utilized as flower boxes and playground novelties.

Finally, our inspection of "satisfactory financial records" and a "positive" income statement led us to a trio of real prizes. One was a shoe box half-full of carbon copies of receipts spanning several years and suggesting an annual gross income of well over one thousand dollars! From it we were able to put together a list of names and addresses of previous clients whom we hoped to contact and persuade to return.

The second was a fairly well-maintained reservation book of customers who had already booked for the coming year. We figured this out not from receipts or any official documentation, but from names scrawled in pencil into the book. It was a coil-bound collection of pages divided according to the cabin name and date. So, we supposed, the name Smith located under Aspen cabin on a specific date indicated that customer Smith would arrive on that date and expect those accommodations. Without phone numbers, addresses or indications of a deposit having been made, we assumed that the camp would receive its first paying guests on the long weekend in May. As we had no way of confirming this, it was clear we would need more than just a little luck as well as hard work in the coming months before we could proudly hang out the sign that read "Glimpse Lake Lodge under new management."

The last of the three "discoveries" was a ledger of sorts. It appeared to be very old and judging from the mould, stains and musty odour, had sat dormant for many years. Inside was a comprehensive diary from the 1930s and the faded writing revealed a riveting history. It was an account of Glimpse Lake when it was a commercial fox farm! Each page represented a different year and was divided into columns tracing the lineage and ancestry of each pair of foxes. Among other things, it outlined the number of kits born to each female, the quality of the pelts, and the diseases and other disasters that befell the ranch. It was written by Bob and Helen Albrecht, the founders of the fox farm and what later came to be known as Glimpse Lake fishing camp. As I pored over it that night, I realized I had unearthed a priceless treasure.

The cold weather and deep snow prevented us from finding the property lines that day, so at dusk we wearily returned to our vehicles and made our way home. Although our hopes were not shattered, they were seriously diminished. We knew we could replace the boats and supplies and we knew we could clean, repair and paint the cabins and main lodge. We also knew we could provide the work for we had the manpower, enthusiasm and determination. The unknown factors were whether or not we could do it all in a relatively short period of time and lure back some of the previously discouraged customers. Imagine our shock when every cabin, boat and campsite was reserved by opening day three months later! We were about to take our place in the history of Glimpse Lake, a legacy started so many years before by a Swiss fox farmer and his young bride.

4

The Early Days

I never met Bob and Helen Albrecht. In fact Helen Albrecht died on November 15, 1970, years before I discovered Glimpse. Although I tried, I was never able to locate Bob. All I have is a faded picture of a lanky and wrinkled elderly fellow sporting a stubble of a beard and smoking a home-rolled cigarette. Helen (nee Graham) and Bob Albrecht were devoted to Glimpse Lake. They called it "a paradise separated from the rest of the world by 4000 feet and a few gates." The passion they held for this land must have, I believe, equalled or even exceeded my own.

Helen, it is said, had a great appreciation of beauty. All through her life, the simplest things and forms of nature; the birds, the wild flowers, the fields, the forests and the mosses were her love. She knew how to find beauty, joy and delight in them all. Perhaps this is why our paths crossed and our destinies were each shaped in some way by Glimpse Lake. It seems I was meant to tell her and Bob's story.

The first time I ever heard of Helen and Bob Albrecht was on the morning of my first visit to Glimpse Lake in 1975. I had wandered behind the old barn to the back meadow where the most noticeable landmark in the vicinity, a huge ponderosa pine, stood like a sentinel over the homestead. Drawn to it, I noticed a weather-beaten sign nailed to the trunk. It hung askew, at a drunken angle, well above my reach. When I looked closely, I could see that it was actually a plaque, in the shape of a shield, which still bore the remnants of faded yellow, red and blue paint. A tattered plastic flower, a bluebell I think, was jammed into a ragged split in the bark just above the plaque. I remember thinking that its artificiality seemed vulgar, although the flower was likely placed there with tenderness, love and sincerity. Words, mostly illegible, and their letters peeled bare by time, divulged that once a poem had been etched meticulously upon the warped plywood surface of the plaque. Only the title, Vaya Con Dios, a few faint scrawls and the poet's name, Helen Albrecht, could be read with the unaided eye. It was a farewell from Helen; maybe her parting commemoration when she was forced by failing health a few years earlier, to leave her beloved lake and move closer to the town of Merritt.

That spring of 1981, Helen's spirit seemed to call me once again. Over the decades, boxes of accumulated paper, files, clothing and probably garbage, had been "stored" in the recess created by the main staircase of the lodge. One of the first tasks when we took possession was to clean up this most obvious threat, assuming, rightly so, that it posed a fire hazard. In no time, we had dragged out a huge pile of material from the cavernous stairwell and piled it by the door to be taken out and burned.

A single sheet of paper, one of hundreds like it strewn on the floor, was slightly separated from the rest. Unlike the others, it was folded, yellowed and crumbling with age. Opening it, I read the following carefully typed poem, which, when I checked, was identical to the memorial plaque on the aging pine tree.

AFTER

Let me go out with no heart-breaking keening
Drifting adown the corridors of Death
In a long shiver through the cypress greening.
Flowers if you will: Poppies to deep my sleeping
Red ones and white, a petalled sacrifice
But wet them not, I pray, with your weeping.
Say, if you must, that you will miss my laughter.
But keep it in your heart as laughter still,

Nor waste a grief I shall not know hereafter.
I will not stir, in cerements faintly musted
In the dim aisles of Oblivion where I rest
Though your voice call me—most Beloved and trusted.

—Helen Graham

Directly beneath Helen's signature was a postscript, written in slightly shaky handwriting, which read: "In remembrance to old friends, from Bob." I assume that after Helen's death, Bob had sent copies of the poem to their friends as a final farewell. Helen had clearly touched the hearts of many, but none more than that of her grieving husband.

Though misty-eyed and somewhat depressed following this emotional onslaught, I vowed to find out more about Helen and hopefully, some of the history of Glimpse Lake. Re-energized, I combed the archives of the Merritt newspaper and contacted local ranchers and neighbours in person, by phone and by letter. I found many facts and seemingly disjointed details, which, when woven together, created an absorbing though sketchy tale of Glimpse Lake and the Albrechts in the early twentieth century on the Nicola Plateau.

The original lodge was built about 1916 by William Hawkins, who was a rancher and probably the first settler in the area. Some time afterward, the property was bought by Stanley Kirby who, like Hawkins, raised horses. Around 1920, Kirby lost the ranch. A lawyer from Merritt named M.L. Grimmett foreclosed the mortgage and in 1927 sold the property to W.C. Albrecht, who married Helen Graham a few years later.

Helen Graham was born in 1901 but arrived in the Nicola Valley in the mid-twenties. She grew up in the Canoe/Salmon Arm area and took her teacher training at the Normal School in Vancouver. She then spent a number of years teaching in the Queen Charlotte Islands and Powell River. After a few years in Grindrod and Coldstream, Helen took a position at the Lower Nicola where she met her future husband, Bob Albrecht, around 1927.

Bob had recently arrived from Switzerland. Next to the Lower

Nicola School, he had established a silver fox ranch with animals he had transported from Prince Edward Island. Shortly after, Bob moved the fox farm to Hawkins Lake and property, now called Glimpse Lake. At this time, the Hawkins/Glimpse Lake property was known by many as the Silver Lake Fox Farm, and by some as Lac du Glace.

Early maps show that in addition to these names, Glimpse Lake was also known as Lauder's Fish Lake. It was named after the pioneer ranching family that still farms there, and lends its name to the road that accesses the area. Joseph Dixon Lauder, who established Lauder Ranch, the original homestead, took out the first water rights on the creek in 1877. They are still in force today along with a number of other licences that were purchased by the family in later years.

The area was ideal for farming for many reasons. On the rolling, grassy plains of the high country, horses could be raised economically and pastured with ease. This was necessary, because in addition to their usefulness as a mode of transportation, when slaughtered, the horses provided most of the food for the hungry foxes. Also, the relative isolation of the location provided a geographical barrier that prevented the foxes from contracting many of the diseases that decimated their populations occasionally and threatened the survival of the business.

Soon after their marriage, Helen joined Bob at Glimpse Lake in 1931 but in 1934, in the midst of the hardships of the Great Depression, they moved the foxes back to Lower Nicola. A victim of human vanity, the farm eventually became unable to sustain itself economically. For many years, fox and mink fur collars were the ultimate in the world of women's fashion. When the trend changed, the business became unprofitable and the suppliers became the casualties. Such was the fate of the fox farm and it was forced to close following this fashion shift. The record book was discarded uselessly under the stairs. With the demise of their fox farm and livelihood, Helen and Bob were forced to find another way to make ends meet. Then they came up with the idea of taking in guests and creating a fishing camp at Glimpse Lake. However, there was one major obstacle to this innovative plan. There were few, if any, fish in Glimpse Lake!

After an unseasonably wet year in 1904, the original dam on the outflow creek from Glimpse washed out. It was essentially nothing more than a beaver dam raised by a John McRae in 1886 or earlier to run a water-powered sawmill on the Lauder Ranch. Apparently most fish were washed away and most of those that remained in the lake died. It was rebuilt by William Lauder soon after but another thirty years would pass before the first large fish was again caught in Glimpse Lake, thanks to the efforts of Bob Albrecht.

In 1934, Bob took it upon himself to stock not only Glimpse Lake, but also Blue Lake, a small, deep body of water a few miles north of Glimpse. He accomplished this tedious and seemingly impossible task by stocking the lakes with fingerling trout, which he caught with a hook and line from the Salmon River. The river was twelve kilometres away and the round trip took a full day on horseback. Bob would leave early in the morning with a collection of four-gallon tin containers strapped to his horse. Arriving at the river, he then hooked the small trout and transferred them to the containers, which he had filled with water. When he had caught enough, he began the long trip home and emptied the surviving trout into the lake. Although such activities are highly illegal today, for good reason, Bob's determination is a classic example of innovation and survival.

Both Glimpse and Blue provided rich environments for the feisty strain of Kamloops trout and they thrived, providing not only a thrilling sport but also a healthy food source. In the summer of 1939, lured by the high country, the old log house on the lake and the need to supplement their income, the Albrechts took in their first guests at Glimpse Lake fishing camp. A fishing retreat, which boasted three boats for the pleasure of its anglers, was born.

It operated only sporadically during World War II, but afterwards, became a thriving business. Some winters Helen returned to teaching and during the 1940s and 1950s she taught in Aspen Grove, Mamette Lake and Lillooet, but she returned each spring and summer to Bob and the glory that was Glimpse. It was their greatest love, a place they always returned to for solace and comfort. It was Glimpse Lake to which they devoted every energy and effort until failing health forced their retirement in 1968.

Those who fished Glimpse Lake in the forties, fifties and sixties speak of it with tremendous awe and reverence. Their tales, etched and carved on the bare logs of the cabins and preserved forever in fading photographs, tell of legendary success rates, both in quantity and size. It was not uncommon to hook trout in the ten- to fifteen-pound range in those days. Even today, there are still large fish in Glimpse Lake, and although they may not be as common as before, they still provide fishermen with a challenge and thrill. Even though there are still those who kill every fish they catch and take them home by the iceboxful, an ever-increasing number of anglers have realized that a delicate balance exists on the lake. To maintain this balance and preserve this resource for the enjoyment of others in the future, the practice of voluntary catch-and-release has been adopted by many outdoorsmen.

Having never met Helen and Bob remains one of the regrets of my life, but I still feel a strange connection to them, possibly due in part to a fascinating and improbable coincidence that came to my attention near the completion of my research. After my father's death in 1999, while going through some of his things, I came across some old pictures including one or two school class photos from his childhood. He had grown up in Westview, a small community on the outskirts of Powell River. Gazing at the picture, I was immediately struck by the youth and beauty of the classroom teacher, who seemed almost a child herself. I was shocked to read, when I looked on the back of the picture, "Miss Graham's class." It seems Helen Graham/Albrecht was one of Dad's primary teachers in the early 1920s! I think she would have been very proud that it was one of her former students who eventually took over the fishing camp after her passing.

As we would quickly discover, we would need every bit of the pioneering spirit that Bob and Helen originally brought to the high country if we were to re-open on time.

5

Outhouses and Insurance Agents

*W*e had established and prioritized a comprehensive to-do list when we finalized the purchase of the camp. There were certain things that just had to be completed. Near the top, catering as we must to bodily functions, were BC Tourist regulation outhouses, as running water was not a luxury available in all areas of the camp. In order to obtain BC Approved Tourist Accommodations designation, it was necessary to conform to the Tourist Regulation guidelines, which included provisions for outhouses. It was a relatively simple task; that is until the government became involved.

So, we obtained the official plans for the construction of an "Outdoor Privy" from the BC Government offices in Kamloops and decided upon ten new ones. We quickly saw the advantages of being able to prefabricate the structures in Vancouver and relocate them at Glimpse Lake once new holes were dug. This we did, following the regulation plans fastidiously. A few weeks later we anxiously awaited the arrival of the government outhouse inspector from Merritt.

At length, late in the morning, a green truck, complete with its yellow government crest emblazoned upon the door, lurched into view at the end of the property. Moments later, it wheezed to a halt in a flurry of dust in front of the lodge. Proudly we escorted the sole occupant of the vehicle, a young attractive woman in a green uniform, to our ten recently located outhouses. She inspected, measured, and photographed each one creating a growing sense of unease and discomfort. Our apprehension mushroomed as the silence lengthened and her scowl broadened. Finally, she completed her last inspection, snapped her clip board shut authoritatively and strode purposefully back to the lodge. Hoping to soften some of the prickly edges, we offered our guest a cup of coffee, awaiting her verdict.

"The holes," she croaked, shattering the silence, "are too close to the back of the wall and the vents require screens."

"The seats, although functional in appearance," she declared, "contain major structural flaws. They are too high and simply not up to standard!"

Aghast, as our modifications needed to be completed before we could open to the public, we stood speechless. Our official opening was only days away. Jack, having taken almost sole responsibility for the construction of the outhouses, allowed a rare scowl of incredulity to betray his concern. He opened the government guidelines and scrutinized the official plan he had worked from. As I confidently assured the inspector that the corrections would be completed immediately, Jack slipped out the side door with his tape measure. Vainly, I argued with the woman that withholding our "approved" designation due to the relatively minor discrepancies that she had identified was both needless and harmful. Moments later an audible "whoop" broke the impasse and Jack burst into the room, grinning from ear to ear. He had been puzzled by the possibility that he had made the mistakes that the inspector claimed. He was meticulous and paid close attention to detail in everything he did. Jack had looked carefully and had discovered that the plans, which he brought for her to see, had been followed to the letter. The outhouses matched the government specifications exactly! Sheepishly, the inspector confirmed Jack's claim. She signed the bundle of documents with a swirl and retreated to her truck, no doubt smarting from a lesson in bureaucratic bungling.

Eventually, as the "biffies" were initiated and put to the test, blocks of wood about six inches high appeared on the floors. They were needed to sit comfortably with feet on the ground, as the seats were far too high for someone of average height. Though the plans were right, they had obviously not been field-tested, prompting Kirsti to quip that they must have been designed by a man!

A few days later we had removed all the wooden rowboats from inside the lodge. They had been stored there for safekeeping but had to be taken out to begin the monumental task of spring cleaning. We soon discovered that this thankless chore had been pretty well ignored for many years. The melting snow revealed the accumulated waste of decades of hoarding. Before it was a fishing camp, the property had served as a homestead and working ranch. Also, being more than fifty kilometres from Merritt, the nearest town, it was remote. Seldom therefore, if ever, had anything been thrown away as it might prove to be useful some time in the future. To us though, it was just junk, so we decided to start fresh with a massive cleanup. For the next three days, a number of huge bonfires burned both day and night, consuming old mattresses, liquids of unknown origin or use, masses of tattered rags, papers and plain garbage. Since then, I have wished more than once that we had taken more care. I am certain that we incinerated some antiques and other valuables. But the need to be shipshape by Victoria Day and the presence of disgusting accumulations of mouse droppings and dead insects tempered the curiosity of even the strongest!

One unexpected discovery was two large cardboard boxes, well sealed and hidden in the attic of one rental cabin. When we looked more closely, we found that they were filled with bags of dried leaves which we tossed on top of the closest fire. The distinctive odour quickly revealed that we had destroyed someone's marijuana stash. Like a bunch of children, we congratulated each other for the help we gave our drug enforcement officers that day! We still have no idea where the stuff came from or who hid the boxes, as no one ever came to claim them.

Late the next morning another visitor from Merritt arrived. Earlier, we had contacted a local insurance agent, being in need of liability and fire insurance. Being unfamiliar with the property, he had volunteered to pay us a visit, take a look at the facilities and provide us with a quote for suitable coverage. Our dedicated crews had been working since eight o'clock stoking the fires, which by the time he arrived at lunch, were reminiscent of industrial furnaces. I had agreed to give our guest a tour of the property. The other partners continued to take apart the aging and hazardous generator shed and feed its oil-soaked and rotting remains to the fire.

Our first stop was the dock, which had somehow survived the winter and still extended precariously into open water. I couldn't coax our guest more than halfway onto the first extension, despite my reassurances of its safety. I had intended to show him that the dock was stable and that our fleet of rental boats was seaworthy. To my great shock, every boat, so carefully launched that very morning, was nearly submerged!

Not wanting to make a mountain out of a molehill, I decided to show the agent our most cozy log cabin. We had recently remodelled it to include a new wood-burning stove and chimney as well as asbestos wall and floor plates. Unwisely, I stepped on the section of the porch that had been routinely dampened by a persistent leak in the roof. I slipped on the greasy moss and crashed unceremoniously to the porch floor, the board disintegrating from the impact. My guest helped me to the main lodge where Kirsti gave us coffee and me, first aid. She had witnessed the entire performance and couldn't stop laughing. Convinced that our application for insurance had been hopelessly compromised, I splashed a generous portion of rum into each cup to soothe our shattered nerves and chalked up the entire event to experience.

The agent left the paperwork on the table, a conciliatory action I thought, and I limped back to his car with him. It was parked in front of the lodge about seventy-five metres from the nearest blaze. Jack, unaware of the previous events, joined us and confidently provided the additional details of other improvements and renovations we planned. Without warning, a rapid series of explosions from the fire interrupted the conversation. As if deaf, Jack continued calmly outlining the detailed plans for addressing safety concerns, as shrapnel whirred through the air and tin cans, smouldering bed springs and melting plastic rained down all around us. Grasping a momentary lull in Jack's explanation and likely fearing for his life, the agent seized my hand, pumped it wildly and wished us a hearty "good luck." He leaped into his car and sped to the safety of the open road, casting a final, furtive glance over his shoulder. Astonishingly, we received a comprehensive policy in the mail a few days later!

After the insurance agent left, we all wandered to the water's edge anxious to find out why our boats had sunk within a matter of hours. The previous fall, the owners had taken the rental boats out of the water and stored them inside the lodge as protection from theft and weathering. We discovered that planks in the boats, being made of wood, had dried out and shrunk when removed from the water. When launched, water bubbled freely through the cracks and splits caused by the dehydration, filling the vessel in no time. Therefore, before they could be used again, the boats had to be re-caulked with putty, re-painted and re-hydrated, compounding our already huge workload.

That evening while discussing the events of the day, we also found out what caused the explosions. It seems several cases of compressed ether, found in the dismantled generator shed and long past their expiry date, had been tossed into the fire. A squirt of ether was used when we needed to coax the temperamental generator to life when it wouldn't start. A full can created quite an explosion when heated. A full case, as witnessed, was a memorable event!

Later, I used this knowledge well when I routinely threw aerosol cans into the bowels of smouldering garbage fires. The explosions they caused stirred up the ashes and provided the fire with enough air to help it burn for many hours. The unpredictable and sporadic detonations also helped to scare away the many pesky black bears that were attracted by human garbage. I didn't really realize at the time how dangerous and foolhardy the practice was. Luckily, no one ever got hurt.

Official opening day loomed ever closer and our efforts became more frantic. We soon realized that regardless of the number of people, the hours in the day or the amount of money spent, there was never enough. There was always something else to do.

Recognizing our inability to do everything that first year, we shortened our job list, focusing on those most essential to facilitating the smooth, daily operation of the camp. In addition to placing the new outhouses, we bought basic utensils, buckets, bedding and cleaning supplies and repaired or replaced a number of roofs, floors, stoves and chimneys. We stuffed additional layers of caulking and countless issues of the *Kamloops Daily News* liberally into the largest gaps between the logs, window sills and cracks in cabin walls. The boats were re-caulked, re-painted, re-nailed and re-supplied with both oars and oarlocks that would hopefully hold up against the combined abuse of the clients and the elements. Also, at the most remote corner of the property, we had a backhoe dig a long, deep trench where we could dump our garbage, fish offal and the odd dead cow.

It seemed that each year, one or two head of diseased or injured cattle from one of the surrounding ranches would "pack in its scrubber" and die on our property. The first time this happened was the weekend before opening day! I was inspecting the bloated carcass where it had fallen near the campground and Jack commented, "Well, it is a pretty place. If I was going to die, this would be the perfect place to do it!"

We didn't want to upset the campers who were expected the next week, so we had to get rid of the remains. I contacted John Lauder, the rancher who owned the cow, but he was unconcerned and had no intention of wasting his time to drag it away. This meant we had to. Looping a few coils of rope around its head, I dragged the grisly mass behind the truck to a well-hidden valley about three miles away, confident it would decompose naturally. During the next few weeks the carcass attracted probably every raven, coyote and black bear in the vicinity. After that we decided just to use the garbage trench, where the remains could be buried, if it happened again.

In addition to being the final resting place for a cow, the trench served as a firepit where we could burn garbage safely in the name of conservation as well as to discourage the ever-present scavengers. This was crucial because guests did not like bears and even a rumour of bears being sighted would often result in the camper leaving earlier than planned.

We were fortunate that the Glimpse Lake property was one of very few large free-hold properties still available, the rest being government leases. It covered over 160 acres, which included a year-round stream, considerable forest growth and almost five thousand feet of water frontage.

Near the entrance was a spectacular waterfront campground. It occupied an expansive, picturesque, flat area. Its shore was free of reeds, allowing easy access to the water by boat. It was also near the best fishing grounds. Sprawling over at least five hundred feet of lakeshore, a certain degree of privacy and comfort was guaranteed. It had no running water, sewage or electrical hook-ups, and created the impression of being in the wilderness. It could easily hold over fifty units if required, but like the rest of the camp, had fallen into a sad state of disrepair. We managed that spring to make some cosmetic improvements, building picnic tables and firepits in about twenty of the most popular locations. We left the remainder to the resourcefulness of more creative campers. Part of the cleanup involved felling dead trees for firewood, safety and general tidiness. Attention to this detail was to prove very fortunate in future years when forest fires threatened our boundaries or when the violent wind and snow storms snapped the conifers like toothpicks.

These and countless other events, both hilarious and tragic, formed the Glimpse Lake experience, moulding and enriching my relationship with Kirsti and the kids. I believe it is mainly from these roots that our mutual respect, friendship and love has flourished. I could ask for nothing more.

6

Row, Row Your Boat

*O*ur fleet of rental boats was a haphazard collection. There were two eight-foot plywood punts and half a dozen ten-foot clinker-built rowboats. In addition, there was a third type that I had never used before but which I had seen on other lakes. It was constructed entirely of pine boards and seemed quite seaworthy.

Oars powered all the boats. Gas engines were banned from the lake and electric trolling motors were new to the market. As well, they were largely unreliable and totally beyond our budget. Each boat was numbered and paired with a set of oars that almost defied description. They were split, taped, nailed and repaired in every conceivable fashion. It was the exception rather than the rule to find a pair with serviceable oarlocks.

We became very concerned for the safety of our future customers when it became clear that the wooden boats that comprised our "serviceable fleet of rental craft" were largely death traps. They all leaked, some more than others. The flimsy seats could shatter without notice and there was often more rot than solid wood in the ribs and gunwales.

The plywood punts had simply decomposed when the frigid temperatures of winter crystallized the tar holding the patches to the bottom. Then, the water soaked into the hulls turning them into a soggy mess. The first guest to rent one that year had put his entire foot through the hull. So, taking no chances we converted the punts into playground toys and window boxes. The other boats were a different story. They needed work, as they had just been overlooked for too long, although they could probably be salvaged.

This was a relatively simple task with a couple of the lap-strake or clinker-built boats. Each board of the hull overlapped the leading edge of the next; hence the term lap-strake. Often, just a liberal application of paint or putty would stop potential leaks. However, the majority of these boats, which were originally very finely hand-crafted from yellow or red cedar, were disintegrating with age and neglect. We decided to make the necessary repairs as well as we could and try to coax one more season out of them while we went searching for replacements.

Because the clinker-builts were real rowboats in the true sense of the word, they were a treat to navigate. Their lines were graceful, majestic and truly enhanced their function. They could be manoeuvred with ease, would glide effortlessly through the water with a single stroke and were resistant to the effects of gusty winds because of their weight. They were also very stable, making them ideal for fly-fishing. Unfortunately we couldn't find a commercial replacement and actually considered making a fibreglass mould from our best remaining boat to take copies from.

We forgot about this idea when we heard about George Procter, a boat-builder from Vernon. He was the man who had built our third type of boat and remarkably, he was still taking orders!

We already owned six of these "Procter" boats which were twelve, fourteen or sixteen feet in length. They also rowed very well, but because they had flat bottoms, did not quite match the performance of the clinker-built rowboats. They, too, were very heavy but once moving, were very functional. Unfortunately, they had also suffered the same fate as the others and had dehydrated badly, creating gaps between the boards large enough to put a small finger into. A coat of paint or a dab of putty was not enough to solve these problems, so we needed to actually stuff the cracks with a rope caulking compound driven into place with a wooden maul. Then we were able to paint over them. Only after this task was completed, could the boats be re-floated. The caulking was amazingly efficient, and if kept in the water, the boats required little maintenance and lasted for a number of seasons without attention. As a result, we decided to order a number of new boats from George and put them into service immediately.

I volunteered to fetch the new boats and deliver them to the camp. I arrived at George's house, located in the Mabel Lake Valley just outside of Lumby, late one May evening. Pulling into his driveway in my Nissan pickup truck, I was greeted by an overly affectionate dog and a stubborn flock of chickens that narrowly evaded an untimely death under my tires.

The screen on the back door of the farmhouse creaked open noisily and an elderly farmer dressed in dusty work clothes and faded suspenders greeted me. He was quite thin and short but wiry. His rugged face was covered in wrinkles and a few scars. Clearly he had experienced years of hard work in the outdoors. Many of his fingernails were cracked and some had a tinge of black and blue from errant blows of his hammer. The thumb of his right hand bore a vivid scar. When I asked what happened, he told me that it was the result of a slight mishap that occurred when he was blowing up a logjam with a few sticks of dynamite a number of years earlier.

While setting the charge, he had accidentally driven a large sliver of wood, over a quarter of an inch thick, through the heel of his hand. It came out on one side of his thumb and broke off, which was fortunate as he would have been stuck there when the dynamite blew. Returning to his workshop, George removed the jagged splinter by clamping the thick end into his vice and pulling his hand free. He then wrapped the wound in a clean cloth and went back to work, a testament to his resilience and determination. After all, he had promised to have a couple of boats ready for delivery in a few days' time and a man couldn't go back on his word, he had explained.

With an infectious grin and a wave of his thin arm, he led me through the tall grass in his backyard, scattering the chickens once again, to his workshop where the boats we had ordered were lined up awaiting delivery.

We stacked the four unpainted boats, separated and cushioned with burlap sacks, in the back of my truck and cinched them down securely with rope. I was fascinated that George at his age was still building boats and became curious about the process. My curiosity was all he needed and I was treated to a tour of the production facility and the tale of a most remarkable pioneer. Following George into his workshop, I was transported fifty years back in time and during the next few hours, was treated to one of those special experiences in life.

It could have been a museum of antique hand tools. The fluorescent lights were the only reminder of anything resembling current technology. Bare bulbs dangled perilously from frayed wires that looped between dusty ceiling joists. A couple of incomplete boats perched on the raised bench. Planes, saws, hammers and odd tools of every description festooned the walls and cluttered the floor. Neat piles of seats, ribs, one-and-a-half-inch fir planks and side boards of pine and cedar stood neatly stacked around the perimeter of the shop. They had been pre-cut and planed and were drying out waiting to be assembled to meet the next season's order. The place was heavy with the heady aroma of sawdust and shavings.

George had started building boats as a hobby in the early thirties, almost fifty years earlier, hardly altering his original design since the first one he made. When informed he had built over three thousand boats, I became incredulous. He claimed these were the last boats he was going to make, but I know that he made the "last" boat at least four or five times and he was still building them in the nineties! He just couldn't stop as long as his health and strength permitted.

His main customers were like us, fishing resorts, and almost every camp in southern BC had its share of George's boats in its rental fleet. In fact, his boats have been seen as far away as the Yukon and the Snake River in Idaho. He always had more orders than he could fill and he proudly claimed that no one had ever drowned using one of his boats.

In wonder, I learned about the Procter boat. George chose all the wood from the timber growing on his property and cut it during the summer. He then sawed the logs into rough boards, arranged them carefully to air-dry for a few months. Finally he planed them to the correct dimensions. The planing had to be timed very carefully and completed before the grasp of winter froze the creek that provided the water for his water-wheel. It was the water-wheel that provided the power to drive the plane, the drill press and the saw in his mill! The cost of energy was certainly right.

In addition to the distinctive design of the boat itself, the Procter boat had a unique trademark. Specifically, it was a piece of galvanized tin that covered the point of the bow where the boards were connected to the hand-carved bow-piece. Carefully attached to the top of the metal plate was a metal ring, about two inches in diameter. This ring was installed to provide a secure anchor for a mooring rope. On the surface, this was a simple and dull detail, but I was filled with growing admiration as George related how he had worked every ring by hand in a coal burning forge that he built specifically for that task.

George never liked to build too many boats at a time, as his space was limited, as were the pre-fabricated parts he constructed in "down" times. As a result, when an order arrived, he often worked long hours to accommodate the customer. He was known to work as much as sixteen hours a day, taking time only to eat and milk the cow. His record was four boats in two days, but he determined the average was about ten hours per boat, the larger ones taking slightly longer.

Although some years were leaner than others, George made a fair living with his craft. Between 1956 and 1968, he filled over one hundred orders each year, the maximum being 130 in 1957. His first boats sold for less than ten dollars in 1932 and by the late 1980s, he was still only getting around $125 for them. As he told me, he felt that was a fair value for his efforts, especially considering how much he enjoyed his work.

In 1990, at the age of 85, George completed his last boat for his nephew, Bobby Procter. It was number 3315 and ended a career spanning forty-seven years and ten months. Even today, many of his boats are still in service, a true legacy to a man who refused to succumb to the pressures of modernization.

In the fall of 2003 an entire era ended when George passed away at the age of 98, and although he is gone, his memory will last forever in the "Procter Boat."

Although the issue of the boats was certainly a formidable challenge, it was the lodge, cabins and their contents that really required a minor miracle if we were to open on time; and time was running out.

7

The Gift of Good Neighbours

The camp at Glimpse Lake Lodge consisted of ten serviceable cabins, a two-storey, three-bedroom, hand-hewn log house built as a homestead, a number of outbuildings and a log barn. The cabins, which were rented on a daily basis for between fifteen and twenty-five dollars a night, were basically single-room dwellings. They were made of logs or roughly constructed walls filled with sawdust for insulation. Often, a single light bulb hung in the middle while a wood-burning stove, a table and rickety chairs and one or more large beds filled the interior. They were very rustic; a luxury to some and a burden to others.

At the entrance to the property was an old barn which had outlived its usefulness and was beginning to sag as the logs rotted. Adjacent to it was a small room that had been added on and in which was stored all manner of nails, screws and fasteners. It contained stacks of pipes and other assorted stove parts and it seemed one could always find what was needed if enough time was spent searching through the dusty chambers. The other outbuildings were once functional cabins that had been converted into storage rooms. There was also an ice-house, a shower-house that was gravity fed with cold water from the creek, and a grimy, windowless and well-ventilated shack that housed the generator.

Every building utilized wood-burning stoves. The stove itself was a curious contraption and served many functions. It had four key components: the flat cooking area, the cooking oven, the water-jacket and the firebox. In addition to cooking and providing heat for the room, the stove was also used to heat water. This minor miracle was achieved because water reservoirs were often built and attached to the sides of the firebox. Water was put in the tanks and when the stove was lit, the heat simply transferred. Although the amount was limited by the size of the reservoir, it was still hot water and it would retain its heat throughout the night. A later refinement on this principal was the installation of coils of pipe inside the firebox itself. Water could be run through the pipes very slowly, getting heated from the fire as it passed through. It could then be bled off into a larger tank, greatly improving the amount of hot water available.

In addition to the widely held belief that food cooked on a wood stove simply tasted better than that from a gas or electric stove, they were aesthetically pleasing. They were manufactured in a wide variety of shapes and sizes and often displayed a delicious combination of lines and curves. Perhaps the most pleasing aspect of a wood stove though, came from the addition of nickel, enamel and stainless steel plated ornaments and decorations, which often transformed it into an artistic piece of furniture. Because of their unique design, there is now a great demand by museums and collectors for wood-burning stoves.

A cabin warmed very quickly once a blaze was ignited in the firebox. The damper, which controlled the amount of oxygen to the fire, had to be closely monitored to ensure a uniform temperature was maintained. Too much air would allow the fuel to burn so intensely the heat would drive the occupant outside; too little would extinguish it completely. Naturally, given that even the best of the old wood-burning stoves were not airtight and only a small amount of wood could be burned at any one time, they inevitably burned out during the night. Unless someone was prepared to get up and stoke it once or twice, the fire would need to be re-lit in the morning, a job which always fell to the person who woke up first.

Obviously, there was a huge demand for firewood. Naturally, locating, cutting, transporting and delivering the fuel was a monumental task. At first, we estimated that we would need at least thirty cords a year. Fortunately, three large dead snags well over forty feet in height and over four feet through the butt stood in the nearby meadow and they became the first targets of our chainsaws. Getting enough wood was labour intensive and became our first major challenge.

One evening after nursing aching muscles and blistered hands, we concluded that we would be a lot better off to hire someone who actually knew what they were doing to supply our wood. The problem was heightened by the fact that we had to return to Vancouver to work and our wood supply was very low. We were running out of time and we didn't know anyone in the area. There were only two permanent residents within thirteen kilometres and we had not yet met them.

As fate would have it, the partial solution presented itself the following day when a rusty blue Ford pickup truck ground to a halt at our door. The occupants, Ted and Daphne Grant, our closest neighbours from down the lake, had come up to introduce themselves. Patience, kindness and determination, among many others, would become the hallmarks of the gentle giant who loped spryly from his truck that afternoon and bellowed, "Howdy, I'm Ted."

We were fascinated by our visitors as our quizzical expressions showed, but curiosity quickly overcame surprise and we welcomed them warmly. With youthful agility, Ted circled his vehicle and, bursting with pride, swung open the passenger door.

"This here's m'wife, Daphne," he said, "and we're pleased t' meetcha." We were about to become acquainted with one of life's unforgettable characters. Ted's bone-crushing handshake was the first indication of the secrets hidden within his massive frame.

Ted and Daphne had purchased one of the lakefront lots and built what was then the only year-round habitation on Glimpse Lake. The house was a gothic arch design and was located adjacent to the public access at the far end of the lake. It was unmistakable, as blue smoke constantly curled from its chimney in sharp contrast to seasonal cottages standing stark and cold on nearby hillsides. It was also the largest home in the area with the exception of our lodge.

Inside, it was functional yet cozy, with the sleeping quarters in the overhead loft and the living area on the main floor. The glassed-in sitting room offered a remarkable 180-degree panorama of the lake and the First Nations Youth Camp on the far shore. The walls were neatly adorned with family pictures, hangings and artwork. Antique china, ornaments and other fascinating conversation pieces decorated the shelves. They included Ted's favourite fly and miniature wood carvings he had whittled patiently over countless winter evenings. A small diesel generator provided electricity, water was piped from a well near the lake and heat radiated from the central airtight wood stove. The most memorable aspect of visits with Ted and Daphne, apart from the animated conversation and strong coffee, was curling one's toes into the multi-coloured wool rugs that occupied every available floor space. Even more remarkable was that each one had been designed and hand-hooked, one strand at a time by Ted!

Ted had retired a number of years before he moved to Glimpse Lake, having worked as a faller and in a variety of other occupations in different Fraser Valley lumber mills. His knowledge of the outdoors could have filled volumes. He was an expert at building, repairing, hunting or fishing and would offer a helping hand to anyone in need. It was Ted who was called upon to administer first aid to a guest injured in a propane explosion. With equal skill and dexterity, he measured and felled huge pines and firs. It was Ted who helped organize the work parties to cut the right-of-way to bring electricity to the area. When a freak storm trapped unwary campers under a foot of snow, Ted was there to winch them free, provide hot chocolate and coffee and clear the windfalls from the road so they could leave safely. Ted's watchful eye and helpful nature made him almost a legend in the area, as he had been the saviour of many who had broken down, run out of gas or just become lost.

Ted's fluid movements and youthful face disguised his sixty-five years, though deep wrinkles furrowed his brow. I still wonder if they were caused by hardship and overwork or laughter, as he always had a joke or story to tell. Time had taken its toll in other areas, for Ted was almost deaf from the screaming saw-blades of the mill and his left hand was missing a digit. Two gaping holes stared vacantly from his upper jaw, where years ago white teeth proudly stood guard. Even from a distance, Ted was unmistakable, as he always stood perfectly erect. His stride, seemingly long and lazy, would consume the miles forcing an average person to jog just to keep up. He could endure, and in fact seemed to thrive on, the heaviest work for twelve and fourteen hours at a time, yet still retain his humour and optimism.

This was the man who now stood before us dressed in work boots, clean blue jeans, a red doe-skin work shirt and a black baseball cap. True to character, he was anxious to offer his help if needed. Eager to share our hospitality, we ushered Ted and Daphne into a newly scrubbed kitchen, arranged some chairs around the old stove and shared refreshments. The conversation provided a sketchy but valuable overview of the local history and our other neighbours.

Strangely, just knowing Ted and Daphne were so close if we needed them, gave us comfort and a sense of security. Over the next three years, they both took on increasing roles and responsibilities at the lodge. They were always there for us; they even took vacations in the winter so they could be available when we needed them during the season. It was truly a perfect situation until sadly and quite unexpectedly, Daphne passed away on April 24, 1984. Valiantly, in spite of his tragedy that year, Ted continued to work for us and completed the obligation he felt he had made.

The main problem continued to be getting ready to open in May. Two hours later, Ted and Daphne had been contracted to get our wood as well as complete other emergent tasks during the few weeks that remained before opening. We had found not only a woodcutter, but a part-time caretaker and manager as well! It was a happy group that returned that night to Vancouver.

However, the winds of change were blowing for my family and me. I had accepted a teaching position in Kelowna, jumping at the offer when it was presented. Kirsti and I were confident that the interior of BC held greener pastures so she too resigned and we sold our house! We began making plans to move in the rapidly approaching summer months. The big question was, how could we mesh the move with our obligation to manage the camp?

8

Let the Good Times Roll— Opening Day

We made our first dollar in a most unexpected fashion. With both anticipation and an element of fear, we waited for the Victoria Day long weekend in May. We wondered if anyone would arrive in spite of our almost superhuman efforts. However, our first real customer arrived, unannounced, a couple of weeks before we were due to open.

Although they knew we were probably closed, a young couple drove in from Kamloops on Saturday May 5. They had just been married and were determined to spend their honeymoon at Glimpse Lake. Both newlyweds had spent many fond times at the lake in earlier days and they wanted to start their lives together on the right foot. It all seemed very right somehow, and although we were not officially open, we bustled about and registered them into our smallest lakeshore cabin called "Grouse." From that time forward it would be known as the "honeymoon suite." Two days later, our weary guests emerged, paid us our $50 and departed, thanking us for a wonderful time. Somehow I still feel those thanks were slightly misdirected!

More good fortune came our way when a group of tree planters rented three cabins for the next week. They were working in the area and with the unpredictable weather, needed shelter and cooking facilities. We were quite glad to have paying guests in residence at the camp that week as we all had to return to Vancouver to work. The place would be virtually abandoned except from the odd visit from Ted. Informing the "guests" that they were on their own for the next few days, we also told them they had to obtain their water from the lake as we had not yet figured out how to work our gravity-fed water system.

Arriving the next weekend, I was surprised to see a cast iron bathtub sitting in the middle of the front lawn with a blaze crackling merrily under it. Our guests had discovered an old bathtub in the barn and desperately in need of a bath, decided to heat water, tub and all. They did this by digging a small firepit and placing the bathtub atop the flames. Because of the high conductivity of iron, they modified it further by installing a small wooden pallet on the floor of the tub so the bather wouldn't be scorched. It was an ingenious and efficient system and like a good recipe, the only requirement was to add water.

Soon after the crews arrived at the end of the day, they began their daily bathing ritual. Someone lit the fire and the tub was filled with water dipped from the lake. The first volunteer, a tall girl who was also the cook, stepped forward as soon as the surface started to steam. I recall that she was very slim and moved with surprising grace. She took the elastics out of the tight bun on her head and her long dark hair tumbled free, undulating in the chilly breeze. I should probably have looked away about that time, but my curiosity got the better of me. She tested the water with her hand, scattered the smouldering coals under the tub and placed her toiletries on a small board conveniently anchored at one end. Without hesitation or any measure of modesty, she quickly stripped, placing her clothes carefully on a chair provided for the purpose and disappeared to her neck in the sudsy cauldron! After luxuriating for half an hour, she jumped out, quickly dried off in the near-freezing temperatures and got dressed. Then, she drained and refilled the tub and stoked the fire; a process that was repeated by each of the remaining workers when it came their turn.

When these friendly folks left, we were reminded that the official start to our first season was only a week away. The few reservations we had came via the mail or telephone at Jack's home in Surrey. Most cabins were booked for long weekends, but business was looking bleak for June and the summer. Every cent of income was needed to help pay for the improvements and the mortgage. We had printed new brochures and sent letters to the addresses we found on old receipts indicating that Glimpse Lake was now under new management. We had outlined the improvements and had promised that returning guests would find a clean, hospitable fishing resort dedicated to insuring a relaxing vacation. Although our expectations were high, the reality was that it is very difficult to rebuild a business and it was clear that our facilities were still very basic at best. All we could do was hope that our efforts would pay off.

We had agreed upon a management model that we hoped would suit everyone's needs. The first couple of months would be the acid test, but we all wanted to be there for the first official weekend. Of the eight partners, six were teachers and therefore only available to operate the camp on weekends and during the summer months. Of the two remaining partners, Bruce was a police officer and had some flexibility in taking vacation and days off. My parents, Peter and Hilda, were retired but were anxious to help where they could. As a result, the six teacher-partners created a schedule that saw the weekends and summer being managed by the teachers and the other times by Bruce, Dad and Mom. Predictably, the brunt of the managerial duties fell to the three of them during June, September and October. It was largely through their efforts at these times that our fledgling business gained a strong foothold.

Inevitably, the Victoria Day weekend arrived and somehow saw all cabins and boats rented. The brochures and letters we sent to those anonymous addresses found in old records proved invaluable and we rekindled the interest of many former patrons. Phone calls and letters arrived daily, all of them containing congratulations and words of encouragement regarding our efforts to re-establish the camp. Bruce was able to arrange days off prior to the weekend, enabling him to open the camp and prepare for the expected onslaught.

The hours at school passed excruciatingly slowly that week. We had planned to start the tedious drive to Glimpse at the stroke of three o'clock on Friday afternoon, accompanied by kids, dogs and relatives. If all went well, we would arrive late Friday night and get ready to provide for our guests and create the impression of being experienced fishing camp operators.

Friday arrived and late that afternoon we edged our van onto the congested freeway, clogged with homebound commuters and weekend vacationers. The May long weekend is the traditional beginning of the summer and camping season in BC. As such, anyone who owns a tent, camper or trailer usually takes off on the year's maiden voyage at this time. The predictable result is mass confusion on the highways. Often, the chaos is made worse by the breakdown of poorly maintained recreational vehicles that have been re-activated after the long winter. Painstakingly, we joined this throng leaving the city to "get away from it all."

Our drive was like the Disney classic "Goofy Goes Camping" and it could well have been the template for the cartoon! It seemed that our sons whined, fought and cried throughout the trip in spite of my threats. The traffic was horrendous but we had no mechanical problems and fortunately, we survived. We arrived safely at the lake late on the Friday night of the long weekend, exhausted and bleary-eyed. Aghast, we counted over forty assorted recreational vehicles already in the campground and another half-dozen or so waiting to register at the lodge!

A haggard Bruce was overjoyed at our arrival. His face was a road map of emotions. He quietly retreated to the kitchen, muttering oaths and rude comments about the mental capacities of fishermen. He had been overwhelmed. Being the only person available to help, and unprepared for the volume of business, Bruce had wisely told the campers to find a site and register in the morning. Cabin guests were the priority as we had to show them their accommodations and brief them on the use of the wood stove and the location of water, wood and outhouses.

By midnight, all the other partners had arrived. They immediately pitched in and some semblance of order was restored, lessening the tension we all felt. Dutifully, someone made certain that a supply of "homebrew" was kept in front of Bruce. He was parked comfortably at the kitchen table, staring vacantly ahead in fatigue and disbelief. Others prepared dinner, changed, watered and put the children to bed, or gave out lanterns, buckets and toilet paper to guests or registered newcomers. Our ability to see what needed to be done and do it was another key to the success of our partnership. Even the two oldest boys helped. Armed with flashlights and sensing a financial opportunity, they crept stealthily over the dewy lawn and collected the large, unsuspecting worms or night-crawlers as they were known. These were divided into baker's dozens and placed in earth-stuffed coffee cans, which were sold to optimistic fishermen the following morning. This became a ritual and resulted in a decent profit for the young businessmen over the years.

After the last cabin guest was registered, the power supply to the camp was flashed three times. This was the signal to all that lanterns should be lit because the diesel generator was about to be shut down. With the exception of Hilda and Peter, who stayed in their trailer, the partners, complete with six children and four dogs, somehow found sleeping arrangements in the lodge. This was a very cozy arrangement and at the cost of privacy, very efficient. Where everyone slept that night is still a mystery but fatigue softened the worst mattress, and there were few complaints. Exhausted but cautiously optimistic, we fell into our beds craving the sleep that we all knew would be far too short.

The only real inconvenience about sleeping in the lodge was the lack of indoor bathroom facilities. Therefore, the famous "thunder-mug" became the order of the day. The lodge had two enamel "pot-ties" and they were taken on a first-come, first-served basis. The rest of us had to use ice-cream buckets. Although they were equally ef-fective, the user needed to be much more careful as the plastic was very flexible, especially when warm. As we would soon discover, the ice-cream buckets were easily spilled, especially when held by little boys. Choosing my steps very carefully the next morning, I silently pledged that indoor plumbing would be a priority for the lodge.

Sun streamed into our bedroom at six that Saturday morning as a persistent rap on the lodge door interrupted my slumber. Annoyed, yet eager to discover what the emergency was at such an ungodly hour, I staggered unsteadily downstairs and opened the door. Five or six fishermen stood expectantly in front of me! In unison, each demanded to rent a boat, register, take a shower or buy items ranging from fishing flies to forgotten cigarettes to sanitary napkins! As soon as I had finished helping one customer, he would be replaced by two more. In the midst of the mayhem, the radio phone jangled, demanding an immediate reply. Clutching the hand-held microphone to my ear, I spoke loudly into the radio receiver. The caller disconnected in frustration being unable to hear my garbled responses. I soon discovered that I needed to depress the "talk" switch if I expected anyone to hear me. In effect, I had been talking into the earpiece rather than the microphone! The next call went much more smoothly.

While explaining to a disappointed woman that we did not yet have hot showers, I turned to watch helplessly as John-Erik, a toddler clad in baggy pyjamas, stepped unsteadily down the last stair from the loft. He tripped and fell flat on his face, cutting his chin. The contents of the "thunder-mug," which he happened to be holding at the time, arched toward the customer, splashing unceremoniously atop her designer joggers. Within seconds, a fisherman arrived with a broken oar, while another complained bitterly that his boat leaked and his feet were wet. There I stood, barefoot in a puddle of blood and urine, compliments of my son who wailed in pain. Expectant customers surrounded me and I was still only wearing a thin dressing gown emblazoned with Mickey Mouse. I began to experience serious second thoughts about the fishing camp business.

The moment and the spell were broken by the laughter of Kirsti who, having inched silently downstairs, was quick to see the humour in not only my attire but the whole predicament. She quickly sized up the calamity, took over and defused the situation as only she can do. I was banished to the upstairs to get dressed, the customers were told to return in ten minutes and our son was cleaned up and hugged.

It was an unexpected shock to discover that a fishing camp operator gets up very early in the day and spends every waking hour trying to solve problems. The sign on the front door said "Open at 6 a.m."—that promise was altered anonymously to "Open at 7 a.m." before the day was through!

9

Fishing Camp to Family Camp

The weekend turned out to be a series of similar bizarre crises, made bearable only by the fact that we had so many willing and able helpers. We quickly learned that a full camp was too much work for only one couple to manage. Initially, we anticipated that every weekend would be the same. Luckily, it turned out that the Victoria Day weekend was by far, the busiest one of the year. Fortunately, it also generated the income we needed to begin operations and, in our first year, helped fill us with optimism.

Battling fatigue as well as traffic this time, we drove back to Surrey late that Monday. We were reeling with the mixed emotions from the weekend's experiences. Earlier that day, Hilda and Peter had arrived, as they had agreed to manage the operation from May 19 until the end of June. My dad was a handyman and both Mom and Dad enjoyed socializing. They were more than capable of helping the odd vacationer who might arrive in what we believed would be our "shoulder" period. We predicted that the summer would be the busiest part of the season. That was, we argued, the prime vacation time. Therefore we believed we had plenty of opportunity to organize, make repairs and generally prepare for the anticipated summer guests. Somehow in our haste, we had overlooked the fact that June is the best fishing month on the interior plateaus and we were a fishing camp. This oversight would soon come as a great shock.

With the radio phone working, the weather fair and the fishing good, even a casual observer could see that our venture was enjoying a highly successful beginning. The reservations poured in, the boats were rented and the campground was packed for the remainder of May and all of June. In retrospect, that first spring was the busiest in our seven-year history. Hilda and Peter worked feverishly all week, and by Friday nights they welcomed the other partners who relieved them. Our schedule provided coverage by at least one other partner for Hilda and Peter so they were able to return home on the weekend if they wanted.

The novelty of ownership quickly disappeared, though. Our clients had specific needs and wants and keeping them satisfied was plain hard work. It was both heavy and demanding. The end of June found Hilda and Peter exhausted and eager to return to their normal lives in Kelowna. As we had arranged, each partner agreed to manage the camp for a two-week period during their time off in the summer. Our schedules overlapped to accommodate the needs of wives, children and customers alike. We staffed heavily for the summer, and expected throngs of vacationers only to discover a puzzling phenomenon. After the July 1–4 long weekend, the crowds thinned to a trickle and occupancy, reservations and rentals plummeted, in spite of the perfect weather! What, we wondered, had we done wrong?

Soberly we realized that fishing camps cater to fishermen, and fishing success diminishes drastically as the long, hot days of July and August warm the lake water. For all intents and purposes, most serious anglers had hung up their rods, waiting for the cooler weather of the fall. We were not known as a family or summer vacation resort so no fishermen meant no customers. Frantically, we searched for a solution to the dilemma of how to fill a fishing camp when the fishermen have all gone home.

In addition to the crisis at the camp, my family was in a heightened state of turmoil as we faced a change in jobs for Kirsti and me and a change in schools for the boys. We decided to rent a home at first, as housing prices were declining that summer of 1981 and we were unfamiliar with schools and neighbourhoods in Kelowna. There weren't many places available but we finally found one. The downside was that we had to sign a ten-month lease and we couldn't move in until September. Therefore we decided to live at Glimpse Lake in the interim, starting in mid-July, and run the camp for the rest of the summer.

The long faces of our partners told the story as we arrived that July 14 with our new truck stuffed with six weeks of food, clothes, etc. Despondently we stared at the near-empty reservation book, the vacant campground and the lonely refurbished cabins, wondering about the financial futures that we had all so readily risked. We needed customers badly and so together, we began to generate creative ideas and suggestions that we hoped might produce the much-needed income.

In order to fill the camp after the fishing season, we reasoned, we needed to offer a wider range of services and attractions. This would hopefully appeal to a wider range of people and bring in new business. So, we decided to target the summer family vacationer who, desperate to leave the congestion of the Lower Mainland, was seeking relaxation and comfort in the serenity of the outdoors. We put up new signs on the Salmon Lake Road as well as the main highway between Merritt and Kamloops directing the casual passerby to our "family campground." We distributed brochures at sporting goods stores, tourist bureaus and just about any public location in Merritt and Kamloops that we could find. We bought advertising in local newspapers and radio stations promoting not only the fishing, which was still quite rewarding if you chose your times correctly, but also hiking, swimming and other family-oriented activities. Back at the lodge, we constructed a group camp area and firepit, children's playground and a swimming float with a diving board, which, unfortunately, sank two months later.

Though we didn't realize it at the time, the most beneficial improvement was the installation of utilitarian but functional flush toilets, showers and laundry facilities. These facilities permitted guests to stay for more than just a couple of days if they so chose. They also appealed enormously, as it turned out, to women. We already knew that, like choosing a house to buy or a place to rent, it was most often the females in a family who made the final decision. Likewise, it was the woman who decided whether or not the campsite was acceptable. Too often we discovered, potential guests would arrive and immediately leave as soon as they discovered that there were no flush toilets or showers. That hardly ever happened after we put in the new washrooms and laundry. Because of hot and cold running water, our clientele expanded significantly. It also made doing laundry, one of our most unpleasant housekeeping chores, much easier.

We wondered how our guests had managed in the past without the luxury of hot water. Kirsti had even asked me once how three or four men, each reeking of fish, could possibly live in a tiny cabin together for a week without bathing and claim they enjoyed the experience.

The washrooms and showers were a great cause for celebration but soon after their completion, a fascinating event occurred. These facilities had been converted from a cabin nearest the main lodge, so for privacy the windows had been painted, boarded over and curtained. However, log cabins tend to be in a constant state of movement and endlessly, it seemed, we were plugging holes and cracks with chinking material. Also, we had installed a very temperamental gravity-fed water system and a propane-fired hot water tank, located directly behind the washrooms. Wind, heat, cold and the odd incident of vandalism wreaked havoc on the very temporary system. It seemed that every day we had to repair something.

On one memorable day, a partner who shall remain anonymous, was on the roof of the shower-house completing some repairs and his routine inspection of the water system. Unknown to him, a very shapely woman was enjoying a shower at the same time. In about the time it takes to dress, or slightly less as it appeared, the fully-lathered woman burst from the room, clutching a large towel around her neck with one hand. In anger, she shook her free fist in the air while swearing vehemently at the figure on the roof. Oblivious to the goings on below him, he was blissfully engaged in hammering new asphalt shingles over the damage from a recent wind.

In an effort to top up the water tank, it seems he had also turned off the hot water. Predictably, the occupant of the shower received a frigid shock. The poor woman, wet, cold and entirely convinced our colleague was a peeping tom or pervert, jumped into her vehicle and sped off down the dusty road. We never saw her again!

Through tears of laughter, we lamented the loss of one of our few customers, but remained convinced that the entertainment was worth the lost revenue! When we gathered enough courage to check out the campground that afternoon, we found that the site was vacant. I have often wished that we had had the opportunity to explain the situation. The sad truth is that we had no record of her name or address as she neither paid for her shower or her campsite the night before. She had apparently arrived quite late and not registered and her fate and identity still remains unknown!

By the last week of July the weather had become extremely hot. Our kerosene fridges were almost useless, and we tried without luck to run the electrical generator long enough to keep the ice frozen in large chest freezers. Valiantly, the old diesel engine laboured to deliver between 90 and 110 volts, causing the appliances to break down, taxing our resourcefulness further. During the hot weather, ice was in great demand by our campers, sparse as they were. We discovered that if campers needed to leave the lake and go to town for ice, they often did not return and we lost a customer. Therefore we had bought a freezer and a large quantity of ice, planning to run the electric generator only long enough each day to keep the ice frozen. It didn't take a genius to see that the cost of running the generator greatly outweighed the profit from ice sales. Inevitably the bags of ice turned to bags of water, regardless of how long the "genny" chugged along. We were faced with the annoying task of driving early each morning to the nearest ice vendor in Quilchena, twenty-five kilometres away, and buying enough ice to meet the daily demands of our guests. Clearly, this couldn't go on forever.

The solution was hidden in the dark recesses of the abandoned ice house, which had sat useless for a number of decades near the lakeshore. In the past it seemed, ice had been stored in the dilapidated structure. On the wall, a pair of long-forgotten rusty ice-tongs hung expectantly. Beneath the floor were a variety of rusted bucksaws and hook-like devices secured to long poles. Our research uncovered the fact, supported by faded black and white pictures found in the lodge, that the supply of ice for the year used to be cut by hand in the dead of winter from the lake once it froze. Using the long bucksaw, large cubes of ice weighing hundreds of pounds and often two to three feet thick were hewn from the middle of the lake. The blocks were pulled from the hole by horses and dragged along the surface to the ice house where they were stacked and covered with sawdust. As there was no electricity or refrigeration, this was the only way to cool and preserve food during the hot summers. Initially, we actually ridiculed the short-sighted pioneers and were sceptical of the process, certain that the ice would melt long before the summer was over. Shortly, we would learn to appreciate not only the ingenuity of the earlier settlers but also the efficiency of proper insulation.

As an experiment, we unloaded part of the next truckload of ice into the shed and covered it with generous layers of sawdust, curious to see how much faster it would melt than the blocks we left in our "freezer." Two days later, after once again discovering a freezer full of plastic bags containing water, I dashed to the ice house and brushed off the thick sawdust layer. Expecting to find a soggy mass of plastic and mud, I was over-joyed when I peered into the gloom. I found intact blocks of ice encased in a fine layer of frost!

To our great surprise, our ice remained cold, hard and frosty even during the most sweltering days that summer. Suddenly, keeping things cool was no longer an issue, and as long as the drinks were well iced, the campers stayed. Even when we hooked up to electricity years later, the ice house stayed in use and did so until the snows of a particularly harsh winter collapsed the roof. Sadly, the caretaker decided to "clean up" the place with a match and a gallon of gasoline, finishing its years of productivity.

During the "ice crisis," I was advised of another alternative to electrical refrigeration. One of our guests was an elderly gentleman who was always anxious to recount one of the seemingly endless tales of his Air Force experiences in World War II. Inadvertently, I had mentioned to him our problem with the ice and he launched into what I believed was a tall tale, though it made for a good yarn.

His large eyes twinkled as he reminisced of the days when he was based with the Flying Tiger squadron in Burma. He was part of the ground support crew, he claimed, and while they awaited the return of the fighters that were assigned to protect the DC 3 cargo planes flying over the Himalayas, they had little to occupy their minds. The humidity and heat of the jungle was overbearing and a cold beer was a rare luxury. Necessity being the mother of invention, the crew experimented with a variety of techniques, trying to find a way to cool the beer when no refrigeration or ice was available. One day, he blurted out, they found the answer!

I became curious and I asked him to tell me about the process. First, a number of bottles of beer were buried in a shallow pit of sand. Then, the sand covering the bottles and the ground adjacent to it were soaked with a few gallons of gasoline or diesel fuel. After waiting a few minutes for the fuel to seep down into the pit, the whole area was set on fire. Eventually the bottles could be recovered from their graves after the flames died out and the ground cooled. The grizzled war veteran claimed that rapid evaporation caused by the fire frosted the bottles and made the contents deliciously cold!

I didn't want to appear too gullible nor display my limited knowledge of physics, so I left our guest before he could launch into another story. Being curious, I thought that I might try this experiment myself on the next trip to our garbage-burning area. My chance came the next day, so following his directions to the letter, I dutifully dug a hole, buried some cans of beer, poured on the gas and lit it. Either I misjudged badly or the story was a set-up. Two cans exploded in the heat, the others were too hot to touch when I recovered them and all my facial hair was singed to charcoal-black stubble! I decided the ice house was the best bet.

Finally we were able to boast that we were truly a family campground and not just a fishing camp. When people arrived, they were able to relax, keep clean, keep food and drinks cold and keep children occupied. What more could one ask of a vacation?

Our strategies began to work and an increasing number of first-time visitors began to appear, lured by the promise of something for everyone. The only complaint seemed to be the long, bumpy and often dusty drive in from the main highway. More than thirteen kilometres of gravel road had to be negotiated before the lake loomed out of the tall pines at the top of the plateau. More than one customer commented that on their first trip to our lake, they actually wondered if they had been tricked by a cruel joke, as the drive seemed interminable.

They say that half the fun is getting there, so in order to deal with the fears and concerns of our first-timers, we decided to put up signs along the road showing the distance left to drive to the lake. In addition, in a rare display of wit and humour, we put up a variety of other signs such as "Railroad Crossing Ahead," "Slow to 80," "Bump Ahead" and "Freeway Ends." We had made the tedious drive into the camp an adventure and, for the weary traveller, it seemed to pass much more quickly. In addition, this simple distraction created a hidden benefit. For some reason, it made customers feel more welcome when the road finally ended at the camp.

One never got bored at Glimpse Lake, as nature provided a seemingly endless parade of treats for every sense. For a family anxious to get away from the city, Glimpse Lake was, and still is, a remarkable wilderness destination. The air is fragrant, clean and energizing. The lake is pristine, with abundant wildlife, thanks largely to the regulation that no gas motors are permitted. The choking blue smoke, greasy oil slick and incessant roar of two-cycle engines is virtually unknown at Glimpse. There are times it seems you are the only one left in the world. The distant crescendo of a blue grouse beating its wings in a mating ritual is as common as a siren in the city. On any day, one can observe an osprey dive and capture a careless trout, a beaver attend to its lodge or a mallard hen and its brood of hatchlings paddle in the reeds.

The forest itself is an adventure playground for old and young alike. The trees are home to a wondrous array of birdlife including woodpeckers, finches and owls. Sightings of moose, deer and black bear are common. An overturned rotten log can reveal a colony of ants or termites or a nest of wasps. Wild huckleberries, salmonberries and mushrooms provide a smorgasbord for those who know what to look for.

In June, as the ground warms and the soft rains of spring sprinkle the rolling hills, a fantastic transformation takes place. Almost magically, the forest floor and grasslands become a tapestry of wild flowers. In a most remarkable display, and seemingly over night, the landscape becomes a painter's canvas. For a few days each year, the pale blues of lupin, the reds of paintbrushes and the pastels of wild columbines blend together miraculously to create a breathtaking explosion of colour.

At dusk, the spectacular sunset signals the onset of nighttime. The absence of any light other than from thousands of stars, which arc in a broad, dazzling band across the zenith, makes the darkness nearly absolute. Yet when there is a full moon, one can often read by its light. It is not uncommon to see an avid fisherman standing in his boat casting a fly at midnight! The mournful hoot of owls, the cries of distant coyotes and the natural harmony of toads, tree frogs and crickets is a sleep-enhancing drug. On very rare occasions, when there is no moonlight and the skies are clear, the aurora borealis can be seen clearly, dancing and flashing crazily on the northern horizon.

A leisurely row or paddle around the lake in the spring or summer is an exhilarating experience for the nature lover. At one end of the lake there is a dam that was constructed a number of years ago to provide irrigation for the farms in the Salmon River valley below. The old shoreline is now flooded and under five or six feet of water, making it a fertile garden of weeds, rushes and reeds. Consequently, it is home to a wonderful variety of waterfowl, insects, reptiles and small mammals. The remains of the old fence posts, "the stakes," can still be seen under water in the middle of the lake between the two largest reed beds. They are also the final resting place of many lake trolls and other assorted fishing gear; silent reminders of scores of unwary fishermen who, for a moment or two at least, were convinced that they had finally caught the biggest fish in the lake.

The thick, floating mats of meshed reeds are a perfect nesting ground for ducks, grebes, red- and yellow-winged blackbirds and loons. A careful excursion into the weed beds will often reward the patient observer with a glimpse of families of newly hatched birds.

Owls, ospreys and other raptors are the natural enemies of the hatchlings and it is not uncommon to see them circling lazily above, anticipating the careless moment when a young bird strays too far from the nest or its protective mother. At such times, nature can be brutal. Like a bolt of lightning, an osprey will streak from the sky, crash into the water and flap away with a doomed chick struggling helplessly in the grasp of vice-like talons. This is a common occurrence, especially among broods of ducks or geese, which often have in excess of eight or ten hatchlings.

Loons, on the other hand, seldom face such overhead dangers because they often only lay two or three eggs, which can be protected much more easily. In addition, chicks are under water much of the time either being fed or learning the skills of fishing from their parents. The main danger to loons often comes from more opportunistic predators like ravens or coyotes. Rather than targeting the hatchlings, these wily creatures focus on the eggs themselves, which can be plundered when the parents are frightened away. As loons tend to construct their nests closer to the shore or even on the shore itself, the eggs are also vulnerable to human intrusion or flooding, which can occur if the lake rises above normal levels during runoff in the spring.

Such natural wonders and environmentally friendly activities began to be the drawing card for Glimpse Lake visitors and gradually we became known as much more than just a fishing camp.

10

Friends and Fine Fishing

*M*emories, like old photographs, are the only things that are left at the end of the day. It is not surprising then, that the memories of the people we met are the most cherished aspects of those wonderful days at the lake. We still keep in touch with many of our old friends, though there are dozens more we have not heard from again. I know that some simply passed away.

On July 31, we received a call on the radio phone from someone wanting to reserve all the cabins and campsites on the far side of the creek. They were concerned that "the sound of partying would not disturb anybody" and wanted to arrive the following day. They planned to stay for two weeks or as long as the weather held.

We had already developed a policy that we would not accept guests who were noisy or who had generators, dirt bikes or anything else that would disturb the serenity. We wanted to be a wholesome family campground and appeal to those who would appreciate the beauty and ecological balance of the area. As Kirsti and I were the only ones running the camp, we were very leery about accepting the reservation. We had visions of wild bush parties and rednecks driving 4x4s. The more pressing problem of cash flow quickly persuaded us to change our minds. We hoped the pending visit by this large group would generate much-needed income and maybe provide a temporary solution to our financial woes. And so it was with serious doubt and concern, that we accepted the reservation, virtually filling our cabins and campground for the foreseeable future.

In the summer, the first tell-tale hint of an approaching vehicle was a cloud of dust that became visible about half a mile down the lake from the lodge. Near lunchtime the following day, I noticed a plume much larger than normal, signalling the first of a convoy of trucks, cars and motorhomes. Throughout the afternoon, the guests poured in. Still somewhat uncomfortable, we politely introduced ourselves as the new owners and directed them to their designated cabin or camping area.

We had turned over six cabins and a large number of campsites to a group that had willingly volunteered that they needed to be separated. More than once, we questioned our sanity. Late that afternoon Kirsti waved me to the window and, a frown of concern etched on her face, pointed to the footbridge. We could see a delegation of eight or ten guests, marching determinedly with drinks in hand, toward the office. Suddenly, we were very aware of our vulnerability and our inability to do anything in the event of an emergency.

Already, earlier that afternoon, we had been puzzled when three or four young teenagers had burst into the office. They eagerly informed us that they had split a large pile of wood, emptied water from some leaking boats and cleared away the encroaching underbrush from the lakeshore near their cabin. This was not how we expected teenagers to behave and we wondered about some other motive as they asked if there was more work they could do! In particular, a handsome pair of thirteen-year-old twins, Mike and Ray Dickens, had asked if they could help collect and burn the garbage. We were even more puzzled when they explained that on previous visits, the owners had let them do exactly that.

However, it was now their parents who stood among the crowd in the cramped office. In their midst was an elderly couple who were pushed gently forward and introduced simply as "Ma and Pa." The room went suddenly quiet and the aging patriarch's voice resonated richly in the close quarters

"Ma and me have been coming to Glimpse Lake for over thirty-seven years," he said, "and we like to relax and have a bit of fun while we're here."

He continued, "We just came over to introduce ourselves and tell you to lock the office door. It's happy hour across the creek and we'd be honoured if you joined us."

So began a friendship with a wonderful group of people who, for the next five years, would stay with us for two weeks every summer. Pa's real name was Stan Forest Sr. and indeed he had visited and fished at Glimpse Lake for the past thirty-seven years. During that time he had seen many changes and he was able to provide us with a wealth of information regarding the history of the property. He had also brought his children, grandchildren and all their friends, in ever-increasing numbers, to enjoy the Glimpse Lake experience. Likewise he had taught them to appreciate its beauty and respect its ecological delicacy.

Following Pa's directive, we locked the door and hung up a sign, which would be invaluable in the coming years. It read, "Gone fishing. Honk in an emergency." Strangely, no one, to our knowledge, ever honked! Accompanying the group across the creek, we joined the rest of the guests on the first of what would become a daily event. It was happy hour; a time to play horseshoes, tell fishing stories, jokes, a few lies and have drinks. Here we also met the rest of the extended family, and within hours, our concerns about isolation and crowd control were forgotten.

During these times Pa told us much about the more recent history of the camp and the surrounding area, as he had fished the lake since 1943. We heard more about Bob and Helen Albrecht and Bruce and Belle Grant and got some first-hand details about the old fox farm. We also learned about the lake being dammed and raised and how the first trout introduced to the lake had been caught in the Salmon River and carried back in buckets.

One night we heard about the old truck that had been rusting in the back field near the swamp for as long as I could remember. Apparently Bob Albrecht had bought it as army surplus after the war. It was an original "Woody"; a Ford panel truck from the 1940s. It still retained its drab, olive green camouflage paint-job but the wooden framework that was responsible for the nickname, had rotted badly. Its tires, though, were still inflated and as I discovered, filled with sand rather than air. Pa said this was routinely done with military vehicles to minimize the time loss and inconvenience of flat tires! The hood protected a flat-head engine that was amazingly intact, in spite of the birds' nests perched on top of it. One day an electrical relay switch from our 1971 Ford work truck failed. On a whim, I replaced it with one from the old Woody, really not expecting much. Astoundingly, it worked! What a testimonial for the Ford company!

The tales seemed endless and we always returned to the lodge in the evening filled with wonder at the determination and persistence of those who, against huge odds, opened up this country so many years ago.

Other than these folks, we had very few guests for the next two weeks. Taking advantage of the enthusiasm and energy of the teenage twins, I was able to tackle many neglected chores. With the boys' help, I was able to find time to bolster the dwindling firewood supply, repair neglected cabins and maintain the dock and aging wooden rowboats. In return, we gave the boys small favours such as a boat to use, souvenir hats and cold drinks. They refused any form of pay, claiming they enjoyed working and helping out around the camp. In addition, my reward came when my daily chores were completed early. When that happened, I got to go fishing!

One would think that the owner/operator of a fishing camp would have plenty of opportunity to enjoy fishing. Unfortunately, the demands of meeting the needs of customers usually prevented such a luxury so the only time I got for fishing was if and when the day's work was finally done. For someone who enjoyed the sport as much as I did, the sight of a fisherman paddling silently through clouds of newly hatched evening insects or the flash of an arcing fly-line catching the final rays of the setting sun was intoxicating and irresistible. But it seemed that no matter how hard I prepared and worked during the day, there was always someone who needed help just when the fish started to surface! This seemed to be my fate.

These special guests though, changed all that. They were the exception to the rule. In no time they learned to look after their own needs! They were experienced fishermen, creative problem solvers and knowledgeable outdoorsmen. If a problem arose, they inevitably took care of it on their own. They really didn't need me at all. In fact, I often called upon one of them to help me when the generator quit or the truck broke down. They were a tremendous help and through their efforts, I too, was often able to join the rest of the fishermen for the most magical time; the evening rise.

The absence of wind combined with the strong rays of the sun that summer caused the top few feet of water on the high lakes to warm very quickly. For a few weeks, the insects were so abundant that the water was murky with their struggling larvae, the surface caked with spent casings and the air alive with hatched terrestrials. Midges, mayflies, gnats, mosquitoes, and damselflies filled the air in such quantities that one could barely breathe without ingesting an insect of some kind. Different hatches occurred daily, depending on the water and weather conditions. As most insects have extremely short life spans, often only a few hours, fishermen had to watch carefully and change their flies when a different species emerged.

For the dry fly-fisherman at Glimpse, though, the true jewel in the crown was the much anticipated appearance of the caddis fly or "sedge" as it is known by many. The sedge exists in many sizes and colours and Glimpse still has some prolific hatches. Early in the year, modest swarms of small caddis flies are common as soon as the warm weather arrives, and can occur at any time of the day. One particular species of caddis fly though, the "travelling sedge," only hatches under very specific conditions at Glimpse Lake. It must be very hot and very calm for an extended period; common occurrences are usually only in late July and early August.

The travelling sedge is a larger member of the caddis fly family, often exceeding two or three centimetres in length. When it pops to the surface, it emerges from its casing and hatches into a moth-like creature with vast, back-swept wings. It then sits quietly for a few moments on the surface of the lake drying off. Without warning, in a crazy, erratic dance, it will suddenly speed across the water, actually creating a wake in its attempt to become airborne. Hence the name, "traveller" or "travelling sedge." These tiny wakes are highly visible and often trigger a feeding frenzy among the trout as well as hungry insect-eating birds like terns and swallows.

Predictably, this hatch also triggers the fly-fisherman, who awaits this evening treat with the joy and anticipation of a child in a candy store. The fishing during the hot summer days can be very poor due to the high volume of natural feed and corresponding lethargy of the fish. But it is not uncommon during a good sedge hatch to hook a fine trout on almost every cast, making this remarkable time the stuff of legends. Consequently, each evening, a flotilla of boats could often be seen rowing out to the weed beds where they anchored in ten to twenty feet of water and lazily threw out a floating line, hoping for an early riser. Usually by the time the rise began, the boats were neatly aligned, about one hundred feet apart from each other, anxiously awaiting the first telltale signs of the coming action. Frequently, tempers flared and people actually swore at each other if one boat encroached into the casting radius of another or if an anchor was noisily thrown into water rather than carefully lowered. As in most sports, there was a code of conduct.

Predictably, the first sign of any pending caddis fly hatch is the marked increase in the activity of birds. Seemingly from nowhere, the sky fills with swooping, screeching night-hawks, terns and swallows gobbling the first airborne insects. Then it is only a matter of moments before the first explosive rise breaks the tranquility, and the hungry trout begin their feast. Almost imperceptibly, tiny rings appear on the water. The sedges have reached the surface and struggle to free themselves from their casings while trying to avoid the predators below and above. Sometimes, one can see small Vs from the dorsal fins of impatient trout cruising near the surface. For a few minutes, the sedges hatch by the thousands, crawling up the fly-lines, flying into faces and scurrying across the water like so many tiny motor boats. The fish, seemingly crazed by the hatch, strike like a hammer, causing many artificial flies to be snapped off or the hooks partially straightened by the intensity of the attack. Satisfied shouts of "I'm on!" echo across the lake, often intermingled with the scream of fly reels as the big ones tear into the backing.

Then, almost as quickly as it starts, the hatch is over. A strange silence comes over the lake as the fish, seemingly responding to an invisible signal, stop feeding. The hum of insects dissipates and the birds disappear. The bite is done, marking the end of another perfect day. The only sound is that of anchors being raised, lines being reeled in and oars dipping into the water as the satisfied anglers head to shore, eager to tell their tales of success and of the ones that got away.

The key to catching fish during the evening caddis fly hatch in the summer is choosing the right fly pattern. The trick is to match the colour and size of the insect hatching at that particular time. An added challenge is to make the fly imitate the action of the sedge on the surface. For the fisherman, a slight breeze is preferable, as it will create a ripple on the water to help disguise the artificial fly. In a dead calm, the fish tend to be much more cautious and selective, as if they are able to tell the real insect from an imitation. At times, though, at the height of the feeding, any dry fly presented in any fashion will catch fish. At others, one can change flies and presentations all night and still not beg a bite.

It also helps to understand the life cycle of the caddis fly. In the heat of the day, the eggs resting on the bottom of the lake will hatch into their pupae form and slowly swim to the surface. Understanding this process increases the chances of catching fish. During this time, a fly pattern that resembles the undeveloped insect, fished on a slow sink or sinking tip line, can be very effective. I have enjoyed fantastic action using a half-back or similar nymph pattern with a very slow retrieve. A nymph especially developed to imitate the Glimpse Lake caddis fly pupae is tied on a Number 8 hook and incorporates a section of orange wool or chenille near the head. I always use this technique in the early evening when there is little surface activity. At this time, though it may appear to be very quiet, fish may be feasting well below the surface on the caddis-fly pupae as they struggle to the top.

A lucky fisherman can easily reach his limit of six in a matter of minutes when the hatch is at its peak. Most conservationists simply release their catches, keeping only those fish hooked too badly to have any chance of survival. Resident loons quickly learn to stay very close to fishermen, as it is much simpler for them to catch the fish that are exhausted after being released. In fact they actually become quite aggressive and are a real nuisance at times. While in her float-tube one evening, Kirsti actually had a large loon swim between her legs which, as can be imagined, created quite a stir!

Another hazard during the late evening is the small brown bat, which is very common and is also attracted by the sedge hatch. Unfortunately, although they hungrily gobble the sedges and mosquitoes, they are unable to tell the difference between the real insect and an artificial fly. As a result fishermen often catch them, usually in mid-cast, creating a very unpleasant experience for both. Often the fly snaps off and the bat flaps off, uninjured. Sometimes though, the hook is well embedded and almost impossible to take out. Rather than handle the bat, I always advised fishermen to just snip off the leader, leaving the fly in the bat's mouth. I think it was probably easier on all the parties.

I became accustomed to participating in this evening fishing with our guests, and unless we wanted to stay a bit later trying to catch the larger fish that seemed to appear just at the end of the rise, dusk was the signal to return to camp. The bonfire was usually kindled and burning brightly by the time we arrived, the tantalizing odour of roasting hot dogs and marshmallows wafting on the cool breeze. It was a memorable time.

Another event, which became an annual custom, was smoking fish on the last full day of the stay. Usually our guests kept only very few fish and many of the smaller ones were saved for the smokehouse.

This tasty treat required a huge investment of time and a considerable amount of preparation prior to the actual smoking process. Before the fish could be smoked, they were split along the backbone and placed in a marinade or brine solution overnight. The brine solution, consisting of coarse salt, dry mustard, spices and often some liqueur, served to determine the flavour of the final product. Those who liked the saltier taste, left the fish in the brine for a longer period. After at least twelve hours, the trout were removed from the solution, patted dry with towels and placed skin down on the smoke rack.

The best smoked trout required a minimum of twelve hours in cold smoke. This was no simple task, for in order to cool, the smoke first had to pass through a long chimney which joined the firepit to the distant smokehouse. It was necessary to cool the smoke in order to prevent the fish from actually being cooked rather than smoked. Although the hot smoke method took much less time, I believe one sacrificed taste and risked illness. This is because hot-smoked fish are not really preserved in the true sense of the word, and they could actually decompose if left to the elements. The smoking process actually cures the fish, allowing it to be kept without refrigeration for extended periods of time.

There are two secrets to successful cold-smoking. The first is in keeping the fire very low and keeping the smoke as cool as possible. The second is removing excess moisture from the fish as the dehydrating process takes place. This is done either by tipping the racks of fish so the moisture will run off on its own or by physically sponging off the juices with a paper towel every few hours. If this step is overlooked, the fish tend to become soft and mushy.

One way of keeping the fire low is to burn green, wet wood and utilize a firebox that has a damper or air control device on it. Constant vigilance is required during the entire smoking process to ensure that the smouldering fire neither burns out completely nor bursts into flame.

Our smokehouse consisted of a four-foot-square wooden structure about six feet high. One entire side was a close-fitting door, which when opened revealed six racks covered with chicken wire, stacked at regular intervals between the roof and the floor. A small vent located near the roof permitted the circulation of the smoke, which entered through the floor from a six-inch underground pipe connected to the firebox twenty-five feet away. The firebox itself was a brick and mortar kiln-like arrangement dug into the bank at the side of the creek. The entrance was a door and damper from a discarded wood stove that could be opened or sealed tight with ease. In the adjacent creek and weighted down by stones, was the fuel. It consisted of thinly split sticks of birch or aspen which, when ignited, smouldered with a pungent, sweet fragrance, but which as any careless keeper of the stove would soon learn, also burned with a vengeance.

The first one up each morning was required to take care of a few morning tasks. Most days, just after dawn, the resident cows would congregate around the lodge, lured by the taste of petunias and the sweet grass of the lawn. Chasing them away quickly became a priority, as cleaning up their "calling cards" was both unpleasant and difficult. Once I had put the run on the herd, I would light the hot water heater, which serviced the showers and laundry, and set the fire in the big main stove in the kitchen.

On "smoking day" my chores also included kindling the blaze that would provide the bed of embers needed for the smokehouse. Then, well before breakfast, people would begin to trickle in with their vats of marinating fish. After a liberal splash of rum in both the brine solution and the morning coffee, we would distribute the fish on the racks, largest ones on the bottom, and label each tray with the name of the owner. It then became my sole responsibility to ensure an adequate supply of cool smoke to the smokehouse and remove the moisture from the fish.

As noon approached, people would arrive with a wide assortment of cakes, crackers and other goodies, which were spread out on the picnic tables behind the kitchen. Sunday brunch was about to begin and everyone in camp arrived at the lodge carrying any food and drink that still remained at the end of their stay. We provided the soft drinks and hot dogs, which added to what was usually a gourmet feast on the communal tables.

After lunch, we tuned in the local radio station from Kamloops, which often picked up a BC Lions football game from the mother station CKNW in Vancouver. The dishes were cleared and the deck chairs erected as the pre-game report crackled intermittently over the unreliable AM waves.

As afternoon faded into evening, happy hour drew near, bottles of wine appeared from nowhere and the smallest smoked trout were removed for "tasters." Kirsti made hot chocolate for the kids, we lit a bonfire and the parents gathered for a final night of friendship and storytelling. The group would shrink, thinned by the inconspicuous exit of the most avid fishermen, determined to have their last "kick at the cat." By dark, the fish were smoked perfectly. I then took the racks out of the smokehouse and wrapped the smoked fish in paper for the grateful customers when they returned from the evening fishing. A bit later than usual, the yawning throng sitting around the fire would disperse. The "goodnights" were reluctantly said and tired but happy campers drifted off for their last night at Glimpse.

The next day became a frenzy of activity as the trucks were loaded, camps were broken and cabins were emptied. We were left with mountains of soiled laundry, truckloads of garbage and almost a dozen cabins to clean. By noon the place was eerily quiet. Tearful farewells had been given and the last vehicle had disappeared over the crest of a distant hill. We were alone again, serenaded now only by the sighing of the wind in the trees and the ripples lapping in the reeds.

It was August and fall seemed to have arrived with the departure of our friends. The signs were everywhere, though we had been able to disregard them in the euphoria of the moment. The green aspen leaves were rimmed with golden halos from an early frost and massive Vs of geese could be seen and heard as they began their annual southern migration. The beaver and muskrats worked throughout the day and night, reinforcing their dens and accumulating stores of food for the coming months when they would be icebound. The days shortened noticeably and the evening breezes, a welcome break from the heat of day during the summer, nipped at the bare flesh. During the day, the smell of woodsmoke and the distant hum of chainsaws suggested that the snows of winter would soon return to the high country.

11

A Penny for Your Thoughts

*A*s I would one day discover, the most important part of effective communication is in hearing what isn't said. By the end of the first summer, in my enthusiasm and determination to make our fledgling business a success, I realized I had neglected the most valuable things of all; Kirsti and the kids.

Somehow, and it was not a conscious decision, Kirsti and I fell into "traditional" male and female roles when it came to work assignments at the camp. I gathered and burned the garbage, sawed the wood and fixed the boats while Kirsti cooked, cleaned the cabins and did the laundry. My jobs took me away for a few hours each morning only to return to the lodge where I spelled Kirsti so she could do the washing and other menial tasks. When she got back, I left to resume maintenance or repairs, leaving her with the kids and guest registration or accounting. In the midst of the constant hustle and bustle, we were never able to leave the lodge at the same time. There didn't seem to be any time left for just the two of us. Even worse, by the time we had finished with the wood, the garbage, the boats, the cooking or the laundry, we were too tired to tend to the needs of our two very active boys. They could find mischief anywhere and needed constant supervision. There never seemed to be enough time for the really important family things like taking curious boys into the swamps to inspect glutinous masses of frog eggs.

Our kids were growing up in front of us and I was missing it. Kirsti could only explain to me the childish curiosity that glinted fleetingly in my son's eyes as a spawning trout briefly turned the creek cloudy with its milt. I was not there to wipe away the tears when a zealous squirrel nipped on John-Erik's tiny finger, mistaking it for a peanut. And I missed the return of five small boys, two of ours and three of Jack's, who sheepishly came home after playing, almost entirely covered in a greenish brown slime. It seems the boys had discovered that fresh cow pies splash when you throw rocks in them!

It had taken me months to discover that we really needed some quality family time together. The empty camp that fall brought an unexpected, though partial solution.

With no camp guests to look after, we decided one morning to replace the "Gone Fishing. Honk horn in case of emergency" sign on the front door with a different one that said "Back in an hour." We all had cabin fever and needed a break. We decided to just lock the door, jump in the truck and drive to the Quilchena Hotel where we could get a hamburger and chips cooked for us and buy some ice cream. On the way back, we stopped to watch a bear amble across a distant hill and a beaver munch on an aspen near the creek. We even paused to swim and shampoo our hair in the Salmon River. We returned to the camp late that afternoon happy, but filled with pangs of guilt. They quickly disappeared as we realized that no new guests had arrived in our absence. That evening, for the first time since owning the lodge, we went fishing as a family!

It was only many years later, in true character, that Kirsti finally confessed how deeply dissatisfied and lonely she was during that summer. Her chores were mundane and boring and being an outdoors person herself, she longed to join me cutting wood or taking care of the campsite. Looking back now, I recognize that a fair distribution of the workload is crucial to the success of a fishing camp. Hindsight is so perfect!

Prior to these events, I had believed that we needed good communications for the safe, efficient operation of the camp. Kirsti had always been a strong and resourceful woman and quite able to look after herself but I didn't like to leave her and the kids alone at the lodge for long. There were times though, that I had to drive to Merritt for supplies or visit a neighbour a few miles away and that could take hours. This was when I always felt a twinge of concern for everyone's well-being as accidents can and did happen.

Earlier that spring, my father had two very frightening experiences. The first happened when my nephew, Aaron, cut himself badly with an axe. He had been chopping wood, under Dad's watchful eye when the blade glanced off a stubborn knot in the wood and sliced through Aaron's boot into his foot. Realizing it would probably take longer to get an ambulance than drive him to the hospital, Dad decided to take Aaron in his car to the nearest emergency room in Merritt. Unfortunately in his haste and heightened sense of anxiety, Dad drove off the road and struck a tree. Luckily, a passerby came to their rescue and delivered them both safely to the hospital from where Dad was able to contact the camp by phone.

The second disaster was potentially more deadly. A guest in the campground had turned on one of his propane appliances, which malfunctioned, leaking gas into the camper. As the guest opened the access panel, the propane ignited, blowing off the door and burning his hands, eyes and face badly. Luckily his fishing partner was able to apply first aid and drive him to the hospital. Although very painful, the injuries were not serious and for the most part, we were told, healed after a few weeks.

Largely due to these very real concerns, we experimented with a variety of communication techniques. At first we arranged that Kirsti would blast an audible signal from an air horn if I was needed back at the lodge. However this tactic was only marginally successful and clearly impossible when I was out of range or earshot. It also startled the guests. If I was fishing on the lake, though, it worked quite well. Observers would hear the blast and then be surprised to see me suddenly lift my anchor, turn for shore and break into a rowing speed reminiscent of the naval battle scene from *Ben-Hur*. The downside was that Kirsti could never be sure if I heard the signal and I had no way of getting back to her if it was me, rather than her that had the problem.

Then we bought a couple of two-way radios, which really

worked well as long as I was within a couple of miles of the lodge. However, they were very heavy and bulky, making them awkward to carry around. Also, they each required twelve batteries that needed many hours to recharge. As we only ran the generator for a few hours each evening, we couldn't charge them fast enough. Using the radios quickly became impractical. Finally, we just got in the habit of telling each other where we were going, what we were doing and when we expected to return. If we didn't get back within ten or fifteen minutes of the agreed schedule, someone would come looking.

Our only reliable link with the outside was the radio telephone. It was also an entertaining and unlikely companion. Cell phones and satellite phones were not yet in use in the early eighties, so any electronic communication was by land-line, or telephone over the traditional wires. There were no lines to Glimpse so the radio telephone was the only alternative. Citizen band radios were options, but their range was limited, the reception was unreliable at best and they could only connect to each other. So, it was impossible to use a CB to call someone on the telephone.

The radio telephone or RT was different. It required a transmitter and receiver for certain radio wave frequencies, which were controlled by a radio-telephone operator. Calls from a telephone could be patched in to RT and vice versa by calling the radio-telephone operator.

To contact Glimpse Lake Lodge from a regular telephone, a caller would dial "0" and ask for the Kamloops radio operator. A typical conversation might start off with:

"Good evening ma'am. My name is John Grain and my number is 536-2174. Would you please connect me with Glimpse Lake Lodge on the 1JL Channel at N699257."

The operator would answer with:

"Just one moment sir. I will see if they are monitoring their phone."

A phone would then ring normally and might be answered with:

"Good evening. This is Glimpse Lake Lodge. Over."

This would be the signal for the person to state their business. After they hung up. the speaker on the RT might say:

"Thank you Kamloops. Glimpse Lake clear. Have a good evening. Over and out."

The one channel and frequency serviced hundreds of customers so conversations became very public. The delicate part was that every customer who was monitoring a radio while waiting for their own call, would hear everyone else's discussion. The only exception to this was if the caller asked the operator to provide "privacy." Privacy was the process of masking the caller's conversation with radio interference. It was not possible to mask the receiver's end, so at least one side of any conversation could always be heard by everyone else on the network.

We kept the RT on at all times to receive cabin reservations. If it wasn't on, we missed the call as there was no function to make it ring like a conventional telephone. Consequently, the rattle of static and the muted, tinny conversations between faceless people were annoying constants.

To place a call from the RT was a greater challenge. The only time the radio operator could be contacted was when the frequency was not being used, which was not often. Therefore we had to listen for the discussion to end so we could get on the line to make our own call. At first, we felt as if we were eavesdropping. Later, we were able to mentally tune out most of the conversations, although they were at times both entertaining and comical.

One dialogue of note was between a woman and her husband, who excitedly confessed that he was coming home a day earlier than expected. This was not a remarkable event until she made the next call to a different fellow right after talking to her husband. We were somewhat aghast at what we heard, along with the other subscribers to the RT network that evening. She told the unknown male that he had better not show up on her doorstep that night because her husband was coming home early. He would, she explained, probably blow off certain parts of his anatomy if he caught them together! How our technology has changed since those days!

By promoting the use of RT and advertising our number

extensively, we received many unexpected reservations for the following year. The fall brought fine weather and excellent fishing so we were very busy right into October. This, combined with the spreading news that Glimpse Lake was under new management, resulted in an unforeseen positive bank balance at the end of the season when we finally latched the doors and prepared for the onslaught of winter.

Each year, Glimpse Lake Lodge closed for the season on the Thanksgiving long weekend. We all gathered on the Sunday for what would become the date of our annual general meeting. At this time we set our goals for the following year, reflected on the events of the previous season and finished the most pressing of necessary jobs. We also prepared a memorable feast of turkey, local duck and grouse for all eight partners, spouses and children.

Thanksgiving Monday was so busy, it seemed to be the shortest day of the year. We had only one day to check out our guests and clean the cabins and campground, drain and winterize the water system and take the boats out of the water. Being unable to afford the luxury of hiring a full-time caretaker, we had to winterize the entire camp and make the cabins and contents as secure as possible so things wouldn't get vandalized or stolen.

During the off-season, we had been told that many people hiked, snowshoed or skiied into the property after we had closed. I suppose they were curious. Amazingly, we seldom had any damage; a remarkable fact given the random and wanton destruction so common in a city. At first we thought we were just lucky, but I think now that it was our foresight in planning for the unexpected. We decided to leave "Cedar," the old log cabin nearest the lodge, open all year.

The high country, like the north, can be both inhospitable and dangerous in the winter and there is sort of an unwritten code that a visitor is never denied food or shelter. Knowing this, we left Cedar unlocked and fully stocked with kindling, dry wood and emergency food supplies such as beans, coffee and sugar. The other cabins were shuttered, locked and bolted. On the door of the main lodge we put up a sign for any visitor arriving while we were away, inviting them to make use of the open cabin. In return, we asked that they leave it in the same condition in which it was found, for the benefit of future guests.

We practised this policy for many winters and there was never a problem with intruders. In fact, being empowered as they were, our non-paying guests assumed a measure of ownership and responsibility for being given the privilege. Each spring we were delighted to discover that the cabin was left in even better condition and even more fully stocked than we had left it. It was always a treat to read the hastily scrawled notes on cigarette packages or cereal boxes thanking us for our hospitality. To those unknown and welcome guests, I send a belated thank you for maintaining the tradition of the "code."

Finally we finished the work and bolted the steel plates onto the lodge windows. A convoy of exhausted owners set out for home, thankful for a successful year and filled with optimism for the next season. The last task was to close the gate and pull the large steel cable across the road to discourage vehicles. With a resounding and sterile "clunk" the massive Yale lock fell into place, ending our first season. Our second year however, was to be overshadowed by a tragedy that would affect me for the rest of my life.

The author's sons, Kristoffer and John-Erik,
return home after the evening rise.

Hiking in the meadow on a crisp fall morning.

Author's daughter Kari playing in a "Procter boat."
Thanksgiving 1986

Author's wife Kirsti puts a fresh coat of red paint
on the doors and shutters.

The barn and corral at Glimpse Lake Lodge in 1950.

The original brochure used to promote the lodge in the late 1940s.

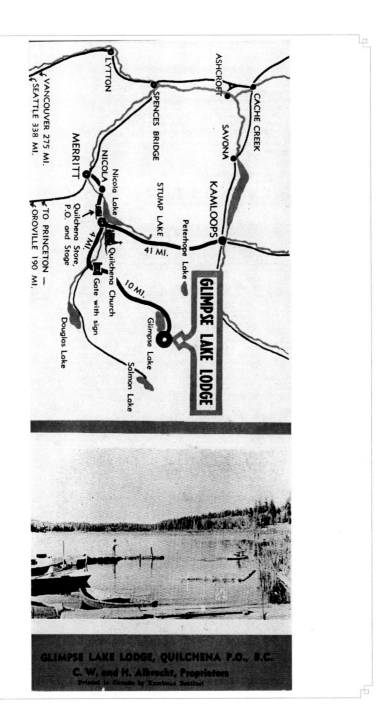

GLIMPSE LAKE LODGE, QUILCHENA P.O., B.C.
C. W. and H. Albrecht, Proprietors
Printed in Canada by Kamloops Sentinel

93

Glimpse Lake Lodge

is no closer to Paradise and dreamland than 4000 feet of altitude, a few gates between us and the world, and a delightful combination of lake, timber and rolling range can take us. But it is rather effective, at that. The mosquitoes and pests are not bad, as the nights are too cold for them.
From mid-June to midsummer, the ranges and forest are abloom with wild flowers. Spring comes late. May and June are early Spring months here, with sudden, changeable weather conditions, and cold when it storms. Grass and leaves appear in June only, but the baking heats of summer find us cool, green, and fresh as an oasis. Fall comes early, with still days, crisp nights and vivid colors, from mid-September to mid-October.

ACCESS: By car, Merritt, 34 miles; Kamloops, 55 miles. Or by stage from Merritt or Kamloops to Quilchena, where met if pre-arranged. By C.P.R. train to Merritt, taxi to Glimpse.

Glimpse Lake Lodge

is no closer to Paradise and dreamland than 4000 feet of altitude, a few gates between us and the world, and a delightful combination of lake, timber and rolling range can take us. But it is rather effective, at that. The mosquitoes and pests are not bad, as the nights are too cold for them.
From mid-June to midsummer, the ranges and forest are abloom with wild flowers. Spring comes late. May and June are early Spring months here, with sudden, changeable weather conditions, and cold when it storms. Grass and leaves appear in June only, but the baking heats of summer find us cool, green, and fresh as an oasis. Fall comes early, with still days, crisp nights and vivid colors, from mid-September to mid-October.

ACCESS: By car, Merritt, 34 miles; Kamloops, 55 miles. Or by stage from Merritt or Kamloops to Quilchena, where met if pre-arranged. By C.P.R. train to Merritt, taxi to Glimpse.

THE ROAD leaves the Merritt-Kamloops highway at Quilchena church. Four miles further, it turns left through a gate with a sign, then climbs steadily through sweeps of open, grassy ranges to the timberline, follows the Lake and ends at the Lodge. It is a country road, now mostly gravelled, and presents no special difficulty or risk to a car. Surface is generally good, the last five miles fair. Chains are not required but it is advisable to have them in the district in Spring and Fall weather.

THE LODGE: A rustic log ranch house, with large verandah facing the Lake. It accommodates 10 guests. The beds are good, inner spring mattresses, and you will sleep well. Fireplace and indoor plumbing contribute to your comfort. The atmosphere is that of a small club devoted to free, lazy summer living and outdoor pleasures. Six hundred acres of private land around the Lake ensure a pleasant privacy.
Many other touches maintain that feeling of a private living, of friendly informality and simplicity.
The board is good, and our dinners are becoming famous and long-remembered—so we are told. The hospitality and welcome are very real, the service attentive and pleasant. Host and hostess do their best to see that you do as you wish, and are happy. Almost without exception our guests have enjoyed Glimpse, and you probably will too.
The nearest phone is 5 miles. Glimpse Lake is ideal for a family holiday.

THE CABINS: There are 6 roomy, clean, log cabins with good porches, for housekeeping parties. Each is equipped with 2 comfortable double beds, curtained off. Utensils, dishes supplied. Bedding not included but can be supplied at extra charge. We also have 3 cabins to accommodate two people each.

SUPPLIES: A small store is kept, but cabin guests should bring their supplies, especially fresh produce, milk, eggs, and bread, as our supply of these is often limited. Canned goods and staples are available at the Lodge, as well as tackle, pop, candy, etc. Nearest stores, Quilchena, 20 miles, Merritt, or Kamloops.

FISHING THROUGHOUT THE SUMMER. Fly and troll equally good. Due to the altitude and coolness, the fishing and fish remain good throughout July and August, with no noticeable off-season. In fact, these months and September bring the best and most enjoyable conditions. The fly starts rather late, and the early season, having few quiet, warm days is often more suitable for trolling.

THE LAKE is one and three-quarters miles long. It is a good, clean sedge lake, clear all summer. The shore presents a happy combination of open and timbered slopes; the bottom, an interesting variety of shelves and bays. Glimpse seems to appeal unfailingly to the sportsman conscious of his surroundings and the quality of his sport.

THE FISH: We boast some of the most beautiful and best-conditioned fish in the Province. There are plenty of fish, in weight up to 10 pounds, average catch running 1 to 5 pounds.
But large and well fed fish are less eager and often take smarter and more patient fishing than small hungry ones. The size of the fish, together with their outstanding fighting qualities and wariness, is the cause of much lost tackle and lost fish, and limit catches are more the result of skill than of luck, but each fish is a prize. Glimpse is a Sportsman's lake. Owing to the small size of the lake, in the interests of fly life and growth of the fish, anglers are requested not to use gas motors.
Tackle for rent at the Lodge.
Side trips to other lakes are easy. Peterhope 11 miles, Nicola 15, Salmon Lake 33 miles.

HUNTING: Mule deer and moose. The Nicola district is well known for its duck and goose shooting. Grouse vary from one season to another. Registered guide.

RIDING: The Nicola Valley has some of the finest cattle country in B.C. The limitless open, scenic ranges, dotted with lakes and aspen groves, start within a mile of the Lodge. On the other side, there are good forest trails. We have quiet horses for children and adults.

SWIMMING season is from early July through August. We have a children's pool and a small beach.

CAMPING: Two fresh, green, and clean campgrounds.

OTHER DIVERSIONS: Rifle range, badminton, croquet, and bowling.

12

For Karen

In September 1981 I started a new job teaching elementary school in Westbank, a small town a few kilometres south of Kelowna, BC. The class was a combination of very capable grade six and seven students and I was excited by the challenge. The school had developed a tradition over the years as both a reward and a recognition for the "graduating" grade seven students. It took them to Victoria in June.

Throughout the year, the school held a variety of activities to raise funds and create a bond among the students. Then, during the first week of June 1982, the two full classes of grade sevens plus my twenty were bused to Victoria where they stayed for three days. They watched the BC Legislature in action, were introduced to their local MLAs and went to the BC Provincial Museum and other educational displays like the Dominion Astrophysical Observatory. As I still had a group of twelve grade sixes to teach, I made plans to take them to Glimpse Lake Lodge for outdoor education when the sevens had gone.

My room-mom was Jackie Johnson, the mother of one of my grade six students, Karen. She organized the transportation and planned the menus with the kids and I took care of the activities. We had a wonderful three days that included inspecting ant hills, building picnic tables and studying the creatures that grew in the swamp water. One night it rained so hard we herded the six boys and six girls out of their tents and "camped" in the lodge for the rest of the night.

When we got back, Karen wrote in her journal that she loved the place and wanted to bring her parents back to go camping in the summer. Her father, Bob Johnson was employed at the Gorman Brothers mill in Westbank. He had arranged to meet his in-laws, the Bentleys, for a family camping trip during his summer vacation. I remembered Karen being very excited on the last day of school in June about maybe making Glimpse Lake Lodge their first stop. That was the last time I saw her.

Karen, her sister Janet, her parents Bob and Jackie Johnson and her grandparents George and Edith Bentley were officially declared as "missing" on August 16, 1982. A search party had been organized after they had not returned from their holiday as scheduled. The police speculated they had been caught in a washout or driven off the road in some inaccessible area of Wells Grey Park. Credit card and telephone records provided no clues and after ten days of extensive searching, the RCMP admitted they suspected foul play.

I joined one of the search parties and combed the Glimpse Lake area. I had hoped that perhaps they had gone to Glimpse Lake as planned but become lost on one of the many back roads. We didn't find any trace of them. By the end of August, the search had intensified and there were reports that the Bentleys' truck had been seen in various other provinces. Composite sketches of two suspects, "persons of interest," were released to the media, but the leads soon dried up.

The resumption of school in September found a grief-stricken staff and student body at Westbank Elementary School. Everyone feared the worst, but hope still prevailed. On Monday, September 13, the police announced that a car, similar to Bob and Jackie Johnson's, had been found in Wells Grey Park. That afternoon, a grim-looking teaching colleague entered my room and told me grisly news. The RCMP had confirmed there were six bodies in the burned-out shell of the vehicle and a coroner had been called in to make a positive identification of the remains. All six had been murdered.

I wept that day . . . for Karen. I wept for Karen's family, for her pain and her innocence and for her lost childhood. I mourned the triumph of evil over virtue and the loss of righteousness and decency. Most of all I cried for a beautiful little girl with an infectious laugh whom I had the privilege of knowing for a mere ten months but who would never fulfill her hopes and dreams.

Months later David Shearing, a resident of the Wells Grey Park area, was arrested and charged with the murders of the six family members. In April 1984 he was found guilty and sentenced to six life terms in prison. He became eligible for parole on November 19, 2005.

After the deaths, a trust fund was established in honour of the slain Johnson/Bentley families. The proceeds of the fund were later used to erect the Johnson/Bentley Aquatic Centre in Westbank. It boasts a large pool, fitness centre and YM/YWCA-sponsored community events; a unique and fitting tribute to a wonderful family.

This shocking event, like so many others in those early years, became etched permanently in our minds. However, time heals all and we once again gradually got used to the different way of life and the routines of camp. People, situations and occurrences that would have previously baffled, confused or shocked us, became commonplace. We just learned to deal with them without fuss or muss. However, it was not just people that presented us with challenges.

13

Bears and Bats

Living in the wilderness, we were constantly plagued with invasions of wild creatures of some sort. Every year seemed to bring a new set of problems. The abundance of insect-life, we concluded, was closely tied to the harshness of the previous winter. Cold weather and little snowfall was certain to kill most of the termites, carpenter ants, pine beetles and other crawly creatures that thrive in the woods. A mild winter with heavy snowfall on the other hand, would guarantee their abundance.

Black bears, though, were immune to the weather and regardless of the conditions, they were our constant companions after awaking from hibernation early in the spring. They would appear, apparently out of thin air, and disappear with equal ease. Whether our guests were camping or renting cabins, they had a universal fear of these un-welcome visitors. Though they seemed to be very large and clumsy, the black bears were as stealthy and silent as cats, making them both unpredictable and dangerous.

In order to discourage them we would try to make certain that food and garbage, which attracted bears initially, was not available in or around the camp. For years prior to our takeover, waste had simply been taken a few hundred metres back into the forest and dumped, making the bear problem worse. It also damaged the en-vironment. So, after digging the new garbage pit, we contracted the backhoe operator to bury the old garbage sites. Then we collected refuse daily and dumped it into the pit where it was burned and buried. This minimized the smells and the potential for attracting roaming bears.

However, the aroma of bacon and eggs cooking over the camp-fire or the stench of carelessly discarded fish offal acted like a bear magnet. So, in spite of our precautions, some bears would return repeatedly. When this happened, we had to call the Merritt Conservation officer, who would bring a live trap in which the bears could be caught. Each time a bear was captured, the officer would attach a tag to its ear. If it was caught three times it would officially be classified as a "nuisance" and destroyed. Others would be driven miles away and released.

As much as we were able to minimize the bear problem, chance encounters with them were inevitable. This was especially true around June when the trout from the lake began their annual migration up the creek to spawn. Bears love fish, and the creek flowed within five metres of our main lodge and through the middle of our cluster of cabins. Once, I was outside the front of the office, chatting with a guest, reassuring him that there had been no bear sightings so far that season. Abruptly, he stopped talking and pointed behind me in disbelief. A small, blonde bear emerged casually from behind the shower-house near the creek and ambled between the parked cars. He ignored us completely even when I shouted and whistled at him. In frustration, I grabbed the lid from a nearby garbage can and launched it at him like a Frisbee. The lid sailed silently over his head, smashing into a nearby fence-post with a loud clatter. He squealed in fright and disappeared into the nearest copse of trees.

Killing bears was the last option if they became a nuisance so we made every effort to chase them away as far as possible. In all the years at the camp, we only had to shoot one. Ted, our caretaker, had been bothered by one particularly aggressive bear that constantly hung around the lodge. It refused to be chased away and once had actually stalked him. Realizing the situation had become dangerous, Ted began to carry his shotgun whenever he left the safety of the lodge. He had decided to kill the ornery critter before harm came to him or someone else. Early one morning after setting the fire in the wood stove in the kitchen, he looked up and saw the bear in the back garden. Snatching up his gun, Ted crept quietly out the back door and walked slowly toward the creek. The bear was nowhere to be seen and Ted cautiously pushed the shotgun's safety to the "off" position. Hearing a sudden commotion, Ted twirled as the rogue bear leaped over the woodpile and charged him. In a single, fluid motion, Ted raised the gun, aimed and fired, hitting the large bear in the chest with a shotgun slug at a range of less than ten metres!

In the summer of 1982 we hired a young man, Peter, to help cut wood and clean the cabins. Near the end of August, he decided he wanted a bear rug, so he bought a hunting licence and a rifle, which he kept in the truck, waiting for his chance. On a hillside near the campground was a large, grassy meadow. I had gone fishing one evening when I noticed a fine black bear uprooting rotten stumps near the top edge of the meadow. We had very few customers, so I radioed Peter and told him that the opportunity had come for him to take his trophy. From my position on the lake, I had a fine view of the bear, the meadow and the surrounding forest. I watched as Peter got out of his truck and started crawling on hands and knees toward the unsuspecting bear. He had gone maybe two hundred metres and was near the middle of the opening when he stopped, kneeled and took aim. A blur of black near the parked truck caught my attention. Another bear, larger than the first, was loping towards its mate—and Peter was directly between them. Although very concerned, I was helpless, being too far away to be heard. I expected the crack of a rifle shot to shatter the silence at any moment, as the second bear came within thirty metres of the young hunter. Still, Peter didn't fire. The first bear suddenly turned and crashed off into the forest. Almost immediately, probably catching Peter's scent, the second bear stopped, spun around and retreated. A few moments later, Peter stood up and walked casually back to his truck.

Anxious to know why he didn't shoot, I rowed back to the lodge, relieved that a beautiful creature had not been sacrificed to become someone's trophy. When I asked Peter, he explained that the bear was too far away and he didn't think he could hit it. Also, whenever he tried to close the gap, the bear moved closer to the protection of the forest. He felt that he needed to be much closer for a certain shot. When I asked why he hadn't taken the second bear, which he could likely have hit with a rock, he replied sheepishly, "What bear?" To my shock, Peter never knew the other one was there!

When we weren't chasing bears in the daytime that year, we were battling bats at night. Aside from the required "thunder mug," the other item of equipment necessary for a restful sleep was a badminton racquet. The main lodge had three bedrooms in the upstairs section of the log structure. Although the chinking between the logs was well maintained, bats, which are able to squeeze into the narrowest crevices, occasionally moved in. The first sign of their presence was the muted squeaking that could be heard when they awoke near dusk and prepared to take flight for the night. Much more unpleasant was the telltale odour of bat droppings, which was both unhealthy and nauseating. Early detection was always the best, because we didn't usually notice the smell until long after the bats had moved in.

The reason for the badminton racquet, though, was that sometimes after the lights were turned off, the bats would emerge inside the house, swooping from one bedroom to another. At first it was absolutely terrifying. Once we became accustomed to the reality of their presence and harmlessness, terror diminished to mere annoyance. Still, it was very unnerving to have a bat flutter past your ear or graze your hair as you lay quietly in bed trying to doze off.

The bat problem was really two problems. First, how could we get rid of the bats once they woke up at night and started their "in-house" aerobatics. The second was how to keep the bats away from the lodge and prevent more of them from getting in.

We tried opening the windows so the bats could escape and we tried catching them in a net, like a butterfly collector might do. They were just too agile and easily avoided us. When all our efforts failed, someone came up with the idea of using a badminton racquet. They were very manoeuvrable and it was quite easy to simply knock the flying bats out of the air as they flew past. Normally we would then release them, somewhat stunned, into the night, though I must admit that in our excitement and enthusiasm, a few died.

Sometimes the bats would come out early and they would be dispatched right away, as they were certain to scare the customers. At other times they would emerge in the dead of night, when everyone was asleep, and someone would have to get up and get rid of the winged intruder. The game of "Bat-minton" was a novelty and quite a source of humour for the public.

One of our guests, a doctor from Washington, was paying a late-night visit to the washroom and witnessed one such event through the undraped windows of the lodge.

Our partner, Jack, was chasing a particularly pesky bat and had turned on all the lights in the lodge trying to find it. The doctor, unable to see the bat from his point of view and totally unaware of what was going on, described a most bizarre scene.

He told of a middle-aged, grey-haired man, dressed in red long underwear, who crept stealthily from one room to another. Suddenly, badminton racquet in hand, the man exploded into a frenzied dance. Like a whirling dervish, he pirouetted, the racquet swathing huge arcs in the air. Then, the flurry of activity would abruptly cease, only to be repeated after the man entered another room. The doctor was certain he was observing the crazed antics of a lunatic deranged with dementia, and was genuinely concerned for his welfare. He was about to intervene and offer his services when, room by room, the lights were turned off. At length, after returning to his cabin, the good doctor fell into a troubled sleep.

Early the next morning, wondering if he had just had some terrible nightmare, he arrived at the lodge, anxious to verify the strange events of the previous evening. When we told him the truth, the lines of concern on his furrowed brow quickly disappeared and were immediately replaced with smiles of relief. He hadn't been hallucinating after all!

We didn't know what bat problems were until the old barn had to be demolished. Early in the spring, the south wall began to sag and the roof drooped dangerously. The barn was almost useless, being nothing more than a storage shed for stove parts and antiquated farm implements as well as a home for pack rats. Once we noticed it was leaning, we were afraid it might collapse unexpectedly and injure someone. Bruce decided to eliminate the problem that summer. With amazingly little effort, he pushed the barn over with a front-end loader, confirming our earlier suspicions and fears. He set fire to the pile of rubble, essentially a mound of kindling, and it burned fiercely until only a large pile of ash and rusted nails remained.

Within days of the barn's destruction, the telltale signs of bats inhabiting the lodge had appeared with a vengeance. They seemed to be living in every crack and cranny of the building. They would even appear inside during the day, flitting through the kitchen or the office. Obviously the barn had been their home and when it was destroyed, the bats decided to move into our lodge!

We had to get rid of the new "guests" immediately and permanently, or the place would soon be unfit for human habitation. We tried to hire an exterminator from Kamloops but that didn't work. They were either too expensive or they wouldn't come to the lake because it was too far from town. We had to find a unique solution.

We tried a number of strategies. At dusk, we would stand guard at the corners of the building with our badminton racquets and try to knock the bats senseless as they came out for the evening. This was no good as the wary bats were much quicker than we were. We tried spraying the cracks with a mixture of vinegar and other assorted foul-smelling cleaning fluids. At first, this chased the creatures away, but the smell quickly disappeared as the liquid dried and the bats returned. On a whim, I tried spraying a can of Raid insecticide into one of the holes and was rewarded with a hum of activity. Almost immediately, twenty or thirty bats flew out in a panic. Apparently they hated the stuff. Moreover, they didn't return when the spray dried! By that evening, I had made the two-hour round trip to Merritt, returning with a case of Raid. With it, I methodically saturated every crack, cranny and opening on the outside of the log structure, chasing away hundreds of the web-winged invaders.

Shortly before dawn the following morning, I quietly went outside, hoping to confirm that the bats had flown the coup. I played the strong beam of a flashlight over the more obvious locations. There were bats flying around everywhere, but they seemed confused. Many more were just hanging on the outside of the logs, but they wouldn't go into the chinking. As it became lighter, they seemed to just fly off into the woods and disappear!

Taking no chances, later that morning, I sprayed everything one more time and to my delight, discovered that not one bat had returned. We had a bat-free lodge once again, which is how it remained thereafter. The rest of the year was relatively uneventful, a welcome respite after the shocking events with the Johnson/Bentley family tragedy. That winter was abnormal in that the temperature seldom went below zero and there was little snow. This brought blessings because the smaller lakes experienced no winter kill in the trout population. However, the lack of moisture in the spring resulted in lower lake levels and increased fire hazards.

14

Carl's Last Cast

*L*ate one hot afternoon in the summer of 1983 an elderly couple in a small sedan arrived and rented a cabin for two days. The man, Carl, had difficulty walking so I helped them unload and get things organized. Our rustic cabins were not equipped with fridges, so iceboxes were used to keep the drinks and perishables cold. Often, the boxes would be left on the veranda, against our advice, and it was common for squirrels, mice, and even dogs, to somehow get into them. Because of this, I reminded Carl to make sure that all his food was inside his cabin at night, and I went to fetch the boat he had rented for the evening. Moments later I heard a blood-curdling scream and looked up to see Carl and his wife moving faster than I thought either was capable of, struggling up the slight rise to the lodge. Thinking someone was injured, I bolted to get the first aid kit only to hear Carl gasp almost unintelligibly, "bear!"

Making sure that neither guest suffered from anything more than fright, I snatched the shotgun from behind the desk and dashed to their cabin. I searched the bushes around the cabin without luck and was about to return when I heard the sound of breaking glass from inside. I peered cautiously into the window and caught sight of a small black bear standing under the table lapping up the milk that he had spilled.

The cabin had two doors, one at either end, so I quietly opened the back door wide and wedged it ajar. Making my way around to the front door, I pushed it open, shouting and banging the butt of the shotgun on the empty garbage can which stood just inside. The terrified bear dashed for his only escape route, the open back door, and disappeared down the bridle trail!

It seems Carl and his wife had been sitting having a snack when he heard a shuffling sound on his back porch. When he opened the door to find out what was going on, the bear rolled unceremoniously over the threshold and landed flat on his back in the single-room cabin. Later we found the shredded remains of a bag of potato chips and supposed that the bear was likely sitting on the porch and leaning against the door as he enjoyed his snack. When Carl opened the door, the bear literally fell into the cabin!

Bravely, in spite of their unsettling experience with our "furry friends," Carl and his wife decided to stay for the night. This would be, I would discover, Carl's last fishing trip. Carl was from Florence, Oregon, where he had operated a fly shop for decades. He had hired American veterans of the war in Viet Nam who were disabled but still able to use their hands. He taught them to tie flies and build fine, custom-made fly-rods, which he sold to customers throughout the Pacific Northwest.

In confidence, Carl's wife told me that he was gravely ill and had wanted to come to Glimpse to go fishing one last time. The weather had been hot and the fishing poor, and I hoped desperately for Carl's sake that things would improve that night. After dinner, I noticed that the boat we had rented to Carl was still tied at his dock, though many fishermen already dotted the reed beds. I checked at Carl's cabin, ostensibly to see if they were okay after the bear incident. When I asked why he wasn't fishing already, he told me he was too weak and in too much pain to get into the boat by himself and row it. When I volunteered to help get him aboard as well as to be his guide and oarsman, I thought he would weep. Within a few minutes, Carl was ready. Jack and I manoeuvred him into a comfortable position at the front of the boat and we cast off from the dock.

Carl advised me to leave my fishing gear at home as he was testing some new rods, lines and flies. He wanted me to try the new equipment and said he would appreciate any comments. We took six new rods ranging from four- to six-weight as well as cases of flies of every description.

I took Carl to a few of my favourite spots and during the next two hours enjoyed some of the most spectacular fishing I had ever experienced at Glimpse, though no one else seemed to be having any success. We hooked many fine fish in the two- to three-pound range and by the end of the evening, Carl's smile seemed to stretch from one end of the lake to the other. Returning to the cabin at dusk, his pain apparently in check, Carl was able to get out of the boat by himself and boasted to his wife of the success and fun he had. As she turned to thank me, the tears glistening in her eyes expressed more than any words ever could.

That was Carl's last fishing trip. He and his wife left early the next morning while I was cleaning the campground. They asked Kirsti to say goodbye to me for them and told her they had left a few things on the veranda which, if we could use them, we were welcome to. Curious, when I got back we both went over to the cabin where a brief note rested on the table thanking us for our kindness. It concluded, "We hope you can use the equipment. We won't need it again."

On the deck were a camp stove, lantern, and icebox. Resting against the cabin wall was a new five-weight fly rod, still in its plastic case, and three wallets of exquisitely tied trout flies, most of which I still have. The next year, we heard Carl had died that September, about a month or so after his visit with us.

15

One Day at a Time, Sweet Jesus

*P*eriodically, skunks would wander through the camp, as would coyotes and other wild animals. Not liking humans very much, most of them would simply visit and then move on if there was no food.

However, in early June of 1984, the telltale odour confirmed our fears that a skunk had moved into the crawl space under Cedar cabin. Therefore, we were not able to rent it out, even though the season was good and we were really busy. I had tried chasing away the skunk, smoking it out and spraying various concoctions around the perimeter of the cabin. But each time, just when it appeared I had been successful and the odour was almost gone, it would return.

One regular guest, Charlie, had been coming to the lake for many years for his annual fly-fishing trip. He had always stayed in Cedar. Right on schedule, he phoned to make his reservation for the following week but I told him why his cabin was temporarily unavailable. I said that he could have another one but he hung up angrily and said that he was not about to change cabins this year.

I hadn't seen the skunk for a long time by the day that Charlie was due and I had almost decided to put him into his traditional cabin. Gazing blankly out of the lodge window over my first cup of coffee that morning, I suddenly saw the wayward skunk, with two tiny kits in tow, making its way slowly toward Cedar cabin. It looked like she intended to make Cedar the permanent home for her family but I wasn't about to let that happen! Putting on rubber boots, rain gear and gloves, I grabbed a freshly painted oar that was leaning against the outhouse, and charged around the corner of the lodge hoping to chase the pests away.

I came face to face with a remarkable sight. Charlie had arrived and he was standing protectively on the porch of Cedar cabin! With a fishing rod in one hand and his net in the other, Charlie was staring determinedly at the mother skunk, which stood motionless not ten feet away. The stalemate continued for what seemed like minutes, though it was only a second or two, neither combatant moving or making a sound. Without warning, a rich, baritone voice broke the silence. Charlie had started singing! The skunk's ears pressed close to its head and the tail twitched threateningly. The kits milled about in confusion. The mother took a hesitant step back, turned tentatively and scampered off into the woods, followed closely by her brood. At a greater distance marched Charlie, who continued with the melodic strains of "One day at a time, sweet Jesus, that's all I'm asking of you." Charlie, singing all the way, chased the skunks far back into the forest. He never got sprayed, the skunks moved out, and Charlie moved in.

Every morning for the next few days, a careful observer might have seen Charlie before he went fishing, gingerly patrolling the outskirts of his cabin. A careful listener might also have detected on the freshening breeze the lilt of a hymn: a song being sung by Charlie asking for "One day at a time, sweet Jesus."

That spring was particularly wet and brought an invasion of wasps, which began to nest in every possible location from holes in the ground to hollows in trees. They seemed to find the spaces between the logs in the cabins especially inviting, so a routine daily task was to go wasp-nest hunting. We actually advised our guests of the problem and being aware of the danger from allergic reactions and the distance to a hospital, an EpiPen was standard equipment in the lodge and the truck.

It got to the point that we couldn't rent the cabins because of the wasps, so we had to figure out how to drive them away. Although I tried the bat solution with spray cans of Raid, it seemed they were too hardy for the non-industrial strength product, so rather than discourage or kill them, I usually just made them very angry. The lumps, bumps and swelling on my hands and face proved that they could fly faster than I could run! We ended up buying a special product, a spray "bomb" developed specifically for getting rid of wasp nests.

The process for dealing with the wasps was a simple but somewhat dangerous task. First, we had to locate the entrance to a nest during the day. Then we "tagged" it with a dab of fluorescent paint so that we could find it once it got dark. This was very important because at night, the wasps were all in the nest and could not or would not leave it to attack their tormentors. Armed with the spray bomb, I would get within a few feet of the nest, shine a flashlight on it and spray a lethal dose of the pesticide into the entrance. Usually, the next day I would find a large pile of dead wasps on the ground below the nest. This was a very effective method of dealing with them and I really gained the upper hand quickly until we discovered the mother of all wasp nests in our attic above the kitchen. It had almost completely encircled the fifty-gallon drum we used to store hot water. It was obvious that a spray can or two of wasp-killer would kill quite a few, but it would only serve to enrage the rest.

To find a solution, we once again turned to the wisdom and inventiveness of earlier pioneers. Remembering how First Nations people would smoke out bees so they could get the honey, we decided to try something similar. Sealing the cracks in the attic from the outside to prevent both the smoke and the wasps from entering the kitchen, we put one end of an exhaust pipe into the loft. Then we attached the other end to the smokehouse and lit a fire in the firebox by the creek. Within minutes, smoke began to fill the attic, making it look like the place was on fire. We continued this for the rest of the day and by nightfall it looked like they had all been driven away.

A few days later, we cautiously entered the attic to see if any wasps had returned. Aside from a few dead ones on the floor, there were none to be seen. So we destroyed the nest and discovered it was even bigger than we had originally thought. Later, when we told an exterminator about it, he estimated that it could easily have held over ten thousand wasps! The wasp problem in the camp largely disappeared with the destruction of the main nest in the lodge, making our lives a little easier for the remainder of the season.

As in any setting where loneliness and isolation are frequent partners, the unwary can unwittingly be robbed of common sense and rationale. Ignorance and the fear of the unknown makes fertile ground for stories and tall tales and, like most areas steeped in history, Glimpse Lake had its share.

16

The Ghosts of Glimpse Lake

Whether they were simply the figments of someone's imagination or the exaggerated creations of explainable events, Glimpse seemed to be haunted by some regular "visitors." Some called them ghosts; others claimed they were the result of excessive drink or overactive imaginations. The locals usually attributed the supernatural events to the restless wanderings of the souls of long-dead pioneers. Regardless, like spectres from history, the sightings were unsettling.

The most notorious of these was the spirit of Jack, the train robber. He was an outlaw at the turn of the century and a most unsavoury character, widely feared for his treachery and ruthlessness. One day, the story goes, Jack's luck ran out after a robbery attempt turned sour. He headed south from Kamloops and was followed to Nicola Lake, where he seemed to just disappear. Determined to rid the area of Jack for once and for all, local ranchers gathered a posse. With a bit of luck, they picked up Jack's trail and pursued him relentlessly into the high country a few miles from Glimpse. The posse, or vigilantes, depending on the teller of the tale, is said to have discovered Jack's hideout, an abandoned trapper's cabin, to which he had fled and sought refuge. The legend claims they surrounded the shack and set it afire, unceremoniously riddling poor Jack with gunfire as he fled the conflagration. Still, the ghost of Jack is said to be roaming the windswept grasslands of the Nicola Plateau, in search of his murderers. Predictably, Jack bears the brunt of the blame when things go awry or events cannot be explained. Cowboys, often jittery after their lonely search for missing calves in the hills in late fall, anxiously tell anyone who will listen about their not-infrequent encounters with the furtive Jack. Even children are warned to eat their vegetables and quickly go to sleep at night, lest the spectre of Jack invade their dreams!

A more credible tale, however, concerns the story of the Lost Fisherman of Glimpse Lake. For years, a story circulated in the small community that a man, a guest of the camp in its early days, had rowed out at dusk for the evening fishing. Many hours after the last vestige of pink had faded from the lingering sunset, he had not returned. In fact he never returned and no trace was ever found of him, his boat or his equipment. Some claim he just stole the boat and skipped out on his bill. But since his mysterious disappearance, many disturbing reports have lingered in the region. Most tell of strange encounters with a man who apparently resembles the Lost Fisherman and "who is looking for something."

The most plausible among them was by one Glimpse Lake resident. He described an event in which a man appeared mysteriously and systematically searched through the tall grass behind his lakeside cabin. When approached by the curious landowner, the stranger mumbled incoherently, but uttered something about needing to find his knife and his fishing rod. He then reportedly turned abruptly, staggered unsteadily down the single-lane gravel track toward the fishing camp and disappeared around the first bend. Almost simultaneously a truck came around the same corner. The vehicle stopped but when the driver was asked, he claimed he hadn't seen anyone! A couple of similar experiences at our camp paralleled this tale and fell into the category of the unexplained.

Late one morning, while removing the garbage from our campground, I was approached by a wild-eyed guest who anxiously began asking questions about "the old guy" who was hanging around the campground earlier. The man, he claimed, wore a ragged fishing vest and tattered cap with flies hanging haphazardly from its brim.

Wordlessly and methodically, he searched through the neatly stacked woodpiles of three campsites. He wouldn't answer any questions when the campers asked him. After a while, being unable to locate what he was after, he just turned and walked away in the direction of the lodge and cabins. Curiously, no one remotely matching his description was a guest of ours and none of our guests, with the exception of the unsettled campers, had ever seen such a person. Nor was he seen again . . . until the summer of 1985.

It was the middle of July and the days were long, hot and very still. The wind, our relentless companion since the first warming rays of sun caressed the frozen landscape in early spring, had finally abated. Good weather was generally the harbinger of poor fishing, as the heat cultivated massive hatches of caddis flies, mayflies and other entomological delights. At last, the fish were able to feast on the over-abundant insect life. No longer forced to compete for food, they became lethargic in the tepid water. An artificial fly, even presented by an expert fly-fisherman, was no match for nature's buffet so fishing success was often quite limited. Our few guests spent as much time enjoying the scenery and serenity as they did the fishing. They relished the long, hot days and they would often spend more time on the lounge-chair than on the water.

Naturally I became curious and quite concerned when, sitting on the front porch enjoying a fleeting interlude of peace and quiet early one afternoon, I heard the muffled sounds of voices raised in anger. They were wafting across the creek from our only occupied cabin. At first I thought there was a marital spat going on and I was reluctant to get involved. So I kept my distance, trying to ignore what was rapidly becoming a heated argument. The conversation ended abruptly and the slam of a screen door echoed clearly among the pines. I was quite surprised when a few minutes later our guests came into view and hurried across the footbridge over the creek. He was a tall, heavy-set man and appeared highly agitated as he approached the office. His long, purposeful strides and grim outlook confirmed that something was very wrong. His receding hairline disclosed a vast network of tiny red veins and capillaries, which seemed to accent his pink complexion and bulging jugulars. His wife, an apparently meek and timid woman, tripped along a few paces behind. I had surmised he had come up on the short end of the argument. I figured they were coming to us for solace, companionship, moral support or a combination of all three. So I prepared to be a good listener, hoping not to become a referee!

With incredulity and dismay, our shocked guest declared, "You will never believe what just happened!" and for the next-quarter hour went on to relate a most bizarre tale. As the story unravelled, I wondered about his alcohol consumption, but there was no smell of booze and his speech was absolutely normal. The fact that his wife kept reinforcing his story with supporting details confirmed he was sober. According to our guest, he and his wife were relaxing on the veranda of their cabin. An elderly man about my build, his fishing hat askew and dressed in jeans and a worn fishing vest, approached them from the lakeshore. He said nothing, not even acknowledging their presence, as he brushed past and barged confidently into the cabin. He made a beeline for the icebox, which he immediately opened and ransacked. Its contents, three bottles of alcohol and a jug of milk, he lined up like soldiers by the sink. Ignoring the shouts of the frightened guests, he methodically emptied the contents of each bottle down the drain and left as inexplicably as he had entered! He then staggered to the dock, where he lumbered dangerously into the twelve-foot boat tied there, cast off the lines and rowed out into the lake.

Turning and pointing to the south, our guest directed my gaze across the lake. In the distance, I could see the boat, which was just a red dot now, stuck in the reeds in Sandy's Bay. From where we were, it appeared to be empty, though it was at least a hundred metres or more from the distant shore. I got a much better look with the binoculars and was able to see that there was no one inside. Thinking the fellow had fallen overboard, I jumped into the first boat I could find at the dock and rowed as fast as I could after him. As I approached the abandoned vessel, I noticed that the shallow water was uncommonly murky. Then I made out what looked like foot prints in the muddy bottom and I could see that instead of swimming, he had waded to shore. I rowed expectantly to the point where it looked like he had pulled himself out of the water and I tied up to a protruding log. I could see a small clearing in the underbrush and tentatively approached it hoping to find the fellow and get some sort of an explanation. I searched the entire area without luck. He had simply vanished!

Returning to my boat, a flash of colour caught my eye. An old hat, crumpled and almost hidden in the greenery perched near the water's edge. The threadbare patch on the front was faded, but close inspection revealed the name brand of SAGE, a well-known high-end fishing rod manufacturer. It was dotted with aged flies, barely recognizable, their hooks pitted with rust. I tossed it carelessly into the bottom of my boat and towed the other one back to the camp, now more confused than ever. When I showed the cap to the cabin guests, they quickly confirmed that it belonged to the mysterious intruder.

Whether it did or not, I will never know, for there were no more such incidents for the rest of the years we had the camp. No one ever claimed the hat, though it hung expectantly for many seasons on a nail in our main office among the other assorted items of Lost and Found. I still have the old hat, one of the few souvenirs I salvaged when we moved out after selling the property. Now it serves as a nostalgic reminder of the wondrous days when I was much younger and more adventurous.

Recently, in one of my more contemplative moments I dug it out of the basement closet and tried it on, finding it to fit like a glove. I showed my wife and, with a twinkle in her eye, she commented, "You know, you look just like that eccentric old coot who scared those people and then disappeared at Glimpse." She reminded me that I also own a weathered and reliable SAGE fishing rod and that my fishing vest is becoming rather tattered. Perhaps old fishermen never die; maybe they just fade off into the mist. Strange . . .

17

Calamity in the Campground

Glimpse Lake Lodge and its office were located at the end of the road, and only reached after driving through the campsite and cabin area. This set-up was different from most resorts and camps where one usually registered, paid and then found a spot to stay. Therefore it was quite possible for someone to set up camp without our knowledge. This created some interesting situations and reinforced on more than one occasion that a good sense of humour and flexibility were mandatory requirements for anyone working with the public.

Our spacious campground was carved out of the natural environment and bordered the lakeshore near the entrance to the property. Rather than having numbers, the sites were defined only by the location of the most recent firepit and picnic table. It was in fact, a bit of a wilderness paradise.

The camping area was flat and carpeted with grass and wild flowers. A small creek, filled with fresh, sweet drinking water trickled melodically through it. Almost every site offered easy access to the lake and campers could keep their vehicles right next to the shore and their boats. That way, a fisherman could leave his rods, net and all his equipment right in the boat without fear of having it stolen. Once launched, three or four good pulls on the oars would put the angler at the drop-off and within easy casting distance of the reeds.

Aging ponderosa pine, spruce and fir trees provided shelter from the pelting rains of spring or shade from the intense summer sun. The forest floor was open and park-like, with hardly any underbrush. Following a shower or a cloudburst, the grassy meadows and moss-covered deadfalls were perfect places to find fiddleheads and edible mushrooms. It was easy to find pine mushrooms, morels and boletus. As always, there was the threat of mistaking a poisonous toadstool for a mushroom, so only the experienced and knowledgeable would actually eat them.

One busy weekend, we discovered that an intruder, obviously camped somewhere else or living in one of the privately owned cabins farther down the lake, was visiting us on a regular basis. Sometime after midnight every third or fourth night he arrived in a pickup truck and helped himself to a load of split firewood that we provided for our campers. Incredulously, in return, he usually left a large plastic bag of garbage which we had to get rid of. He must have been careful with what he threw away because search as I would, I was never able to find anything that would identify him. I even sat in my truck one night until after midnight hoping he would show up. Of course he never did. Oh, how I wanted to return his garbage! As fate would have it, his activities ended abruptly one wild night.

It began as "one of those days." The night had been hot and muggy. By breakfast time, the thermometer had already reached eighty degrees, a condition only experienced during the "dog days" of summer. Not a breath of wind marred the lake's surface for the entire morning and by 10:00 a.m., clouds of damselflies and mayflies exploded from the reeds, exciting the birds into a flurry of feeding. Millions of spent insect carcasses floated limply, carpeting the oily water. By noon, trees on the opposite shore shimmered as the heat created a ghostly mirage. The cattle too seemed uncomfortably hot. They had moved out of the sun and found a dusty wallow in the shade of the cooling branches of the aspen and silver birch. Even the dog was exhausted from the climbing mercury.

There had been no rain for weeks and the BC Forest Service

had advised us that there was a ban on all open burning due to the high forest fire hazard. By early afternoon, the cumulus clouds had begun to build on the surrounding ridges. As the uncharacteristically still day wore on into late afternoon, thunderheads with their telltale anvil structure, encircled the lake like so many covered wagons. The puffy grey clouds thickened to black and seemed to hover over us like hungry monsters. The inkiness began to swirl visibly over our heads as a tornado might, and in the fading light, took on an eerie purple hue.

The stillness and heat were oppressive and it seemed the entire world had gone silent. The odd bold fisherman drifted aimlessly among the reeds. The majority though, had long since fled the lake fearing that their graphite rods might attract lightning. Like our cabin guests, we sensed a momentous event was about to occur. We waited, lounging on the veranda, drinks in hand. In the rising humidity, garments clung like glue to our clammy bodies. An abbreviated twilight turned the premature dusk to darkness. The anticipation, like the air, became electric. Preparing for the worst, we lined up storm lanterns on the tables, located the candles, and gathered emergency firefighting equipment. Finally, we extinguished the throbbing generator as the first rumbles of thunder rolled ominously in the distance and intermittent sparks of lightning, like underpowered flashbulbs, danced on the horizon.

The first breath of air caressed the skin like a silk glove. The pungent tang of ozone came wafting on the freshening breeze as the last vestige of muted sunlight disappeared from the horizon. On the Nicola Plateau, with few trees to hamper its progress, the wind can quickly become intense with the approach of a weather front or summer thunderstorm. It is also very unpredictable; a fact which many fishermen would confirm. As the breeze increased, the temperature plummeted and not knowing what to expect, we became quite worried.

It was on this night that our garbage-leaving firewood thief chose to pay his final visit. It began very gently. The leaves of the aspens rustled like a swarm of approaching locusts and the tallest pines began to bend, their needles sighing and trunks groaning like a room full of old men. The babble of ripples in the reeds quickly became a roar as the wind whipped the surface of the lake into a tempestuous cauldron.

Without warning, the storm struck with its full power, downing trees, ripping asphalt shingles from roofs, and drenching everything in a torrential downpour. A sodden camper, trying to tie down a loose tarpaulin before it was shredded to pieces in the gale, was shocked to hear a crack like a gunshot. Looking up, he stared unmoving as a large branch from a gnarled fir snapped from its trunk and plunged earthward like a huge feathered dart. It landed barely a dozen yards from his site and impaled itself in the canopy of a truck whose driver had just unloaded his garbage and started to fill the empty box with dry Glimpse Lake firewood! Our visitor tried frantically to remove the branch but gave up after a few moments. He climbed into his vehicle and sped off as the intensity of the storm increased. He probably realized that in fact it could have been an entire tree rather than just a branch that hit him.

The next day when we heard the story, we wondered if the trespasser might come back and try to sue us for damages. Just to make sure, we called our lawyers. They advised us that if he tried anything like that, we could simply bring a counter-suit for trespassing and theft. Not surprisingly, the culprit never returned and to this day, I still don't know who it was. I wonder if he appreciates the irony and the poetic justice of the event!

The health of the trespasser or the condition of his truck was the least of our worries that night though. Trees and branches were snapping like twigs from the force of the gale and it became obvious that our campers were in real danger from falling debris. Already, a number of guests had moved their rigs to open ground away from the forest and some tenters had sought refuge in the lodge where it was warm and dry.

Though the rainfall seemed heavy, the forest was still very dry and fire posed the greatest threat. Driven by the vicious winds, lightning could easily ignite a tree, rage into a wildfire and consume our property with ease. Our worst fears were confirmed when a blinding flash momentarily froze the landscape. Almost immediately, an explosion of thunder, the sure sign of a too-close-for-comfort lightning strike, shattered the night.

As children, we were taught to count the seconds between seeing the flash of lightning and hearing the thunder from it. Generally, an interval of five seconds meant that the lightning strike was about a kilometre away. Because the interval between the flash and the thunder was less than one second, we correctly assumed as we had feared, that our property had been hit.

We dashed outside into the pitch darkness and sloshed through the greasy mud, anxious to determine whether a building or adjacent tree had been struck. We didn't have to look far. A bright red glow could be seen from the forest a few hundred metres past the last cabin. With binoculars we could see that the top third or so of a large snag had been blasted away by the impact. Our main worry was that the remaining snag was flaring dozens of metres into the air like an oil refinery torch burning off waste products.

We grabbed portable water pumps, shovels and chainsaws from the lodge and ventured into the forest to find the blazing tree. We had intended to put the fire out and protect our investment but we could not find the tree in the darkness! We were amazed. Although we could see the blaze clearly from a distance, it was simply too dark to find once we were in the forest. Even though the fire burned brightly, its light couldn't penetrate the canopy of foliage. We already had scuffed shins, cuts and bruised hands. We were not willing to risk the accidental loss of an eye, so we decided to wait for dawn, hoping the winds would die and the incessant rainfall would prevent the fire from spreading. By midnight, the wind had eased and the odd star could be seen through breaks in the dark clouds, although showers occurred on and off most of the night.

The next morning dawned fresh from the cleansing rain and the still-damp cabin roofs steamed in the strong morning sun. After a sleepless night, we quickly found where the lightning had struck. The top of the tree was still smouldering and a few others in the immediate area were badly charred. Falling cinders had caused a number of spot fires on the forest floor but much to our relief, there were no flames visible anywhere. An ugly gash two or three inches wide cut deeply through the bark the entire length of the tree. The lightning bolt had sliced the old pine open like a tin can. Pitch flowed steadily from the cut into a small, smoking crater at its base. It was here that the bolt had entered the ground. Miraculously, however, only a small area was affected.

Earlier, we had reported the fire to the Merritt Forestry Service and their vehicles arrived at the lodge later that morning to deal with our fire, one of many that had started during the night. A telltale wisp of smoke curled lazily from the charred snag, which we pointed out to the fire crew. They quickly dealt with it and returned within the hour. We treated them to a hearty Glimpse Lake breakfast as thanks.

Luckily, the fire had not spread during the night, probably due to the persistent rainfall. The crew simply cleared the area of any remaining fuel and decided to let it burn itself out. We were informed, though, that as landowners we were required to take "all possible measures" to fight the fire on the private property. If we had not done so, the Forestry Service had the option of billing us to recover the costs of fighting the fire. This was news to us, and very valuable information of which no one, our neighbours included, seemed aware. Clearly, we were very "lucky campers."

A good storm was always an interesting event and certain to provide excitement. However, excitement often wore different disguises. Soon after the storm and not long after we had finished clearing away the windfalls, a very bizarre event occurred. As we discovered, trees sometimes fall without assistance from the wind and it is true that when a tree falls in the forest, it can be heard!

One of the more unpleasant but necessary chores each morning was to wash and re-supply all the outhouses, most of which were located in the campground. They were set well back from the camp, nestled among first-growth stumps, rotting snags and the remnants of an earlier logging operation. We had discovered that one easy way to get firewood was to clean up the fallen trees and standing dead wood. Therefore, much of the area within the immediate vicinity of the campground was selectively logged and very open. However, we had chosen to disregard one particularly large snag adjacent to the outhouse area, and it stood looming like a beacon. It was over twenty feet tall and at least four feet through the butt. Huckleberry bushes and fir seedlings sprouted from the top. Leaning precariously, it had deteriorated so badly with rot, it was dangerous to fell. Even if we had taken it down, there was probably not any useable wood in it.

It was a calm and beautiful morning and I was in the process of mopping out the first of two outhouses. The other one was occupied by a young woman. The air was warm and the melodious trill of robins filled the air. Suddenly an explosion shattered the serenity and the earth shook so violently I was nearly bowled off my feet. I looked up aghast to see that the other outhouse had disappeared, shrouded in a massive cloud of red dust! I heard a blood-curdling scream and I stood in shock as a terrified woman bolted from the haze. She clutched her jeans protectively around her thighs, and sprinted to her tent.

When the dust—the product of decades of decomposition—settled it was very obvious what had caused the uproar. Without warning or apparent cause the old snag, which must have weighed hundreds of kilograms if not tonnes, had crashed to the ground, missing the outhouse by mere inches. The rotted tree had disintegrated when it struck the ground and, although undamaged, the outhouse had been dislodged by the violence of the impact. Understandably the unfortunate occupant fled in horror! Although they never uttered a word, both she and her husband quickly packed and left that day. They never said as much but I am convinced that they somehow thought that I had engineered the near-tragic event.

Looking back on the close calls, we were very lucky, given the potential for disaster from leaking boats to falling trees to forest fires, that there were so few accidents and injuries on our property.

Many years earlier, Glimpse Lake had been restricted to the use of electric motors only. Banning gas motors on many of the small lakes is one of the many wise regulations implemented by the BC Department of Fisheries and Wildlife. They have also imposed bans on ice fishing in some lakes and put "catch-and-release" and "fly-fishing-only" restrictions on others. These regulations are designed to achieve two goals. The first is to maintain and enhance the wild trout fishery in BC lakes. It is hoped this will provide a self-sustaining recreational activity for many future generations. The second is to foster an appreciation for the natural environment and encourage outdoorsmen to adopt and practise ecologically friendly activities in the wilderness. As fishing, especially fly-fishing, is one of the fastest growing sports in North America, it is BC sportsmen who will undoubtedly benefit the most from these policies. "Take nothing but pictures and leave nothing but footprints" is a guideline we should all consider very carefully.

Some people, though, seem to court disaster and carelessly put themselves in dangerous positions by disregarding advice or instructions. Many ignore warnings of wet paint, or do just the opposite when told to avoid poison ivy, not eat wild mushrooms, not feed the bears . . . or not use gasoline engines on Glimpse!

There is no good reason to use a gasoline engine on Glimpse, because the lake is very small and easy to navigate. Even worse, the oily exhaust and fumes are obnoxious. Signs located at each public access to the lake tell visitors that gas motors are banned and only electric motors are permitted. It is largely because of this regulation that the lake is still productive to this day. I must admit, though, having been caught more than once in the strong winds so common to the lake, that I have sometimes cursed the inconvenience. There are few, if any places on Glimpse Lake to get out of the wind once it begins to blow. In spite of this disadvantage, the avid anglers who frequent the lake value the absence of gas engines. It is simply quieter, more natural and better for the fishing.

Once, in spite of warnings from other campers, an individual chose to ignore the regulations. He was obviously an inexperienced camper. He arrived noisily blaring his horn and shouting orders. Willie Nelson wailed mournfully from the truck stereo, the frenzied dogs barked insanely and the children howled. The mother, clearly drunk, swore crudely at both her husband and the kids. Somehow in the confusion they set up a tent and started an ancient gas generator that wheezed to life and chuffed abrasively. The father manhandled the aluminum boat carelessly off the roof rack and it crashed unceremoniously to the ground. Popping another beer, he mounted the six-horsepower gasoline motor on the transom of the boat. He unpacked his rod and, ignoring his wife's complaints, started the engine and roared out into the middle of the lake where he began trolling.

In no time a group of concerned campers stomped into the lodge demanding that we do something about the offensive camper. When he returned to the camp a short while later, we all met him at the shore. We told him to quit using the gas motor and respect the regulations. When we suggested that he was breaking the law, he bellowed, "I can do anything I bloody well please, so f*** off!" Then he disappeared into his tent. Through the mesh of the tent's doorway, I told him about our camping policy regarding noise and the gas engine. I also said he would be thrown out of the camp if he didn't obey the rules. The only response I got was a loud snoring.

A couple of "regulars" who had been coming to the lake for many years approached me, very sympathetic to the problem. They said that they had seen this sort of camper before. They also were aware that my concern was not only for the lake but also for the fact that customers would simply leave if the camp became too noisy. They reassured me they would take care of any problem, if it reappeared.

When finally the "problem camper" awoke just after his nap, his generator was missing its spark plug and the gas line from the tank to the outboard motor had mysteriously vanished! He immediately confronted his neighbours and accused them of theft, which they denied. In response, our "guest" found a spare gas hose, connected it to the tank and once again shattered the silence on the lake by racing from one "hot spot" to another. Luckily, it didn't take long for him to get hungry. He had also run out of beer so he went ashore well before the nightly hatch, leaving the fly-fishermen to enjoy the serenity of the late evening. Taking no chances though, he locked his gas tank and hose in the cab of his truck, fearing he might be the victim of sabotage again. That night the camp remained quiet as our friends slept off the effects of their alcoholic consumption during the day.

The next day dawned clear, quiet and calm. Just after breakfast I heard the office door slam and a very hungover camper entered demanding service. He was extremely angry and screamed that his outboard motor was missing. He ordered me to return it immediately, convinced that I had stolen it during the night. Denying any knowledge of the crime, I agreed to go back to camp with him and see if the other campers had seen anything. I asked him to show me where he had left his boat for the night, suspecting he had probably hidden the motor himself and in his drunken haze, just forgotten where. A scrap of paper, nailed neatly to the transom of his boat, caught my eye. It was a note which read:

Glimpse Lake is always nice and quiet
We're not accustomed to a riot!
We all come here to fish and sleep,
Your noise and rudeness makes us weep.
Our kind advice you did not take,
Your motor might be in the lake.
But saner heads, though, did prevail.
Your motor sits beneath the rail,
Just behind the Glimpse Lake sign.
You're lucky not to get a fine!
The sign, though, is ten miles away
And so we hope you will not stay.
So pack your bags and get your engine.
Don't wish, or think, or even mention
Your trip to Glimpse, though sad and lonely,
IT'S FOR ELECTIC MOTORS ONLY!

Gravely, I handed the man the note, told him the sign was at the corner of Salmon Lake Road and Lauder Road, thirteen kilometres away and ordered him not to return. I'm told there was great applause and cheering when, an hour or so later, he left.

18

Rustlin' in the Wind

U ntil the mid-eighties, fishing camps in BC seemed to endure a dubious notoriety among fishermen as well as bank-
ers. They had a painfully short season, the best fishing being
only during the cooler months of May, June and September. They
also had a reputation for being rundown, neglected and generally
uncomfortable and dirty. This combination made them difficult to
buy or sell. Financial backing was almost impossible to secure due to
the limited potential for income. Fishing camps were simply not a
good risk and were most often viewed as being a lifestyle rather than
a true business. The sad reality was that we were a fishing camp, and
when the fishing was poor during the heat of summer, the customers
stayed home in spite of our efforts to make it a family destination.

All that changed after 1986 when the Coquihalla Highway was
completed between the Lower Mainland and Merritt. With the cutting of a ribbon, more than a million Vancouver suburbanites were
suddenly within a three-hour drive of what, until then, had been a
relatively remote and untouched wilderness. This new market spelled
new hope for BC Interior fishing camp operators. It promised a longer season, greater demand for accommodations and most importantly, a more rosy cash-flow picture.

Coincidentally, the fledgling concept, "Eco-tourism," had begun
to flourish. In addition to the fine fishing available in the higher lakes

in the summer, the many ecosystems surrounding Glimpse Lake offered a multitude of activities for the adventuresome outdoorsman. Guests had the freedom to hike, bicycle, birdwatch or even pick mushrooms if they chose. As well, the remote interior wilderness became home to a new breed of tourists who simply yearned for serenity, solitude and the beauty of nature. The Nicola Plateau satisfied all these needs. The more inaccessible and lonely backcountry, which had previously only served as range land and cow pasture, had suddenly become a prime tourist destination.

Even today, summer in the high country is an enchanting experience. The long, hot days, punctuated with frequent thundershowers create a fertile growing medium. The gentle, rolling hills are home to a bountiful array of grasses, flowers and succulent flora of every kind. Aspen groves and hidden ponds line the hollows and glens, sequestered between the undulating knolls. In stark contrast, heavy forests of evergreens appear along the ridges, as if from nowhere, and stand guard protectively across the horizon.

The breeze, warm and relaxing, creates the momentary illusion of a seascape, as it surges in waves across the open grasslands, carrying both the seed and scent of countless bouquets. As morning progresses, massive cumulus clouds billow overhead and drift aimlessly across the heavens until they either disperse without ceremony or swell into towering thunderheads in the late afternoon.

The fragrances of newly turned earth, freshly cut hay and pine pitch permeate the nostrils. A careful observer will often be rewarded with a distant flash of movement as a vigilant coyote or hawk pounces on a careless shrew or squirrel. Sometimes the only sound is the sighing of the wind, the drone of a distant chainsaw or the bleat of a lost calf. Sometimes it is so quiet that the beating of one's heart is the only thing that shatters the silence.

However, it was not a beating heart that made me sit bolt upright in bed just after twelve o'clock one July night; it was the sound of a faint but distinct rifle-shot in the distance.

The sound of gunshots in rural areas is commonplace and Glimpse Lake was no different. Farmers protecting their stock from marauding coyotes, hunters in pursuit of birds or big game or simply target shooters could legally discharge their firearms during the day. A gunshot at night, though, usually indicated activity of a more sinister nature such as illegal poaching. Not only was this activity illegal, it was unsportsmanlike and dangerous, as the perpetrator clearly had no respect for the law, private property or the possible consequences of his thoughtless act.

Although the opening of the Coquihalla had increased our business and future prospects, it had also introduced new opportunities for those with darker intentions. Theft and break-ins, previously almost unknown at the lake, had increased significantly as the volume of visitors ballooned. Signs of the city were everywhere as garbage was carelessly discarded and acts of vandalism were committed wantonly.

The single late-night shot and the knowledge of previous criminal activity in the area made me very uneasy, and as I slipped back into a fitful sleep, I decided to phone the police and begin my own quiet investigation at the earliest opportunity.

My restless slumber ended with the sunrise and, with my son in tow the early morning found us navigating the truck along heavily rutted logging roads that meandered through the rugged woodlands to the north of the lake. If I was right, the shot had come from the open range area used by the Douglas Lake Cattle Company to pasture some of their many head of cattle in the summer.

I was not sure what I expected to discover; perhaps the remains of a deer, a moose or a bear. Poachers were normally a lazy, opportunistic group who just took the best sections of the animal, carelessly discarding the rest. The odd case of poaching was usually the result of someone wanting some cheap, easy meat for the freezer. Recently though, a growing black market in bear parts had flourished in Vancouver. There had been a disturbing increase in the discovery of almost intact bear carcasses; animals senselessly slaughtered and left to rot after having their claws and gall-bladders hacked out. It was rumoured that the claws and bladders were dried out and ground into powder to be sold for an exorbitant price as an aphrodisiac.

As I drove along the well-worn gravel road leading to Blue Lake, I encountered a man and woman on their mountain bikes. I asked but they had not heard the shot the night before. They did tell me that in the course of their tour, they had passed a couple of campers at Blue Lake and another tent and truck camped in the large meadow about a kilometre north of the lake. I thanked them, somewhat disappointed that I had found nothing out of the ordinary. The screams of ravens or the sight of circling buzzards would have alerted me to a fresh kill, but there was neither. I didn't even see a coyote. On a whim I decided to take the longer and rougher circle route, which passed through parts of the Douglas Lake property and the First Nations land that bordered the south end of Glimpse Lake.

Bursting out onto the prairie that formed the open rangeland of Douglas Lake, I was struck by the thought that my search was really a waste of time. I could see for ten miles in every direction, but there was only a single potholed path providing access to the entire vast area. Anybody who wanted to hide could easily do so in any of the hundreds of valleys or copses of trees that unfolded in front of me. Everything seemed perfectly normal to me. Nothing seemed out of place and the serenity was completed by the faint lowing of Douglas Lake cattle drinking their fill of water in a distant slough.

Finally, I decided to quit worrying about the gunshot in the night, uneasily aware that even if I did stumble on something suspicious, there was little I could do. I was unarmed and accompanied only by a child. Clearly, I hadn't thought my plan through very well. I was not prepared in any way to confront a poacher who would likely be both nervous and dangerous.

I wound my way back to the lodge by noon and completed the promise I had made to myself the previous night. I contacted the Merritt RCMP by radio phone and told them about the shot I heard as well as my suspicions. I was a bit surprised to learn that they intended to send an officer out to our camp. As well, they would ask the Range Patrol, an organization of volunteer ranchers dedicated to preserving the ecological balance of the plateau, to pay us a visit. I also decided to talk to the Blue Lake campers that the bicycle riders had told me about, just to see if they had heard or seen anything unusual. I was beginning to think that perhaps the shot I heard had just been a bad dream.

After gathering the garbage and dumping off a fresh load of firewood at the campground, I continued up to the Forestry Service camp at Blue Lake. The first person I approached was a young fellow in a camper who had just returned from fishing. He claimed he had not heard any shots at all. Then I spoke with a middle-aged couple whose tent occupied the other site. They were sitting around the campfire, beating off the mosquitoes and enjoying a hot drink. After identifying myself and explaining my concerns about the gunfire, they confided that a shot had wakened them in the night. In fact it had been disturbingly close. They were openly nervous about the situation and were considering leaving the camp that day because of it. I suddenly remembered the tent and truck in the meadow that the bicyclists had told me about and decided to pay a friendly visit.

Cautiously, I guided my truck along the overgrown cart trail that was all that remained of the old logging road leading to the meadow. I was feeling a bit nervous and didn't want to announce my presence unnecessarily. I parked a few hundred metres short of where I supposed the camp to be and approached quietly on foot. Emerging from the cover of the underbrush, I was able to see immediately that the camp was abandoned. The signs of recent occupation, however, were everywhere.

The delicate ground cover had been churned up by spinning tires, leaving ugly scars across the landscape. Plastic bags and broken beer bottles were strewn everywhere and embers still smouldered in a hastily built and largely dysfunctional firepit. I cleaned up the glass and garbage, using one of their discarded bags, and extinguished the fire with water from the manual fire-pump I always carried in the truck. Finally, I pulled out the large spikes, complete with remnants of rope, which for some strange reason had been driven into the trunks of adjacent trees. In less than half an hour I had almost returned the area to its natural state again.

Later, when I thought back about it, I recall being puzzled, though not overly concerned, about a large rectangle of dead grass that had been trampled down. I knew that a tent will often kill the grass because it blocks the sun from reaching it. This particular piece of damaged turf however, looked much more permanent and strangely out of place. Why, I wondered, would anyone set up camp in the middle of a cow pasture. There were dust wallows everywhere, the barnyard stench was almost overwhelming and it was impossible to avoid stepping in the mounds of manure that dotted the area. There was ample camping space at Blue Lake and it was certainly more inviting and picturesque. Heading back to the camp, I felt uneasy. Things didn't add up but I couldn't put my finger on the cause.

The next morning, a blue and white GMC pickup arrived. Out jumped an young man who flashed an RCMP badge from a worn wallet and then asked to rent a boat and go fishing! I had just assumed that any visit by the police that day would have been about yesterday's phone call. Somewhat envious of the apparent "perks" of his job, I gave him a sturdy rowboat and pointed to where he might try his luck.

To my surprise, he ignored my advice and anchored noisily directly in front of the campground, where he took out his binoculars. He made a great fuss of using them to study the ducks and other birds in the reeds adjacent to the camp. Then he put them back in their case and took out his fishing rod. I had made a point of telling the officer that he would be most successful if he tried his luck where the fish were known to congregate. I had also told him to avoid the campground boat-launch area, where he was now anchored!

I had become a bit suspicious as soon as the RCMP "fisherman" had cast off. A fly-fisherman will always set up his rod and tie on a fly so it is available for immediate use. He wants to be ready just in case he comes upon actively feeding fish on the way to his favourite spot. Uncharacteristically, our guest did no such thing but simply rowed away and wasted at least half an hour of fishing time getting set up.

When he finally began casting, I realized what was wrong. Obviously, he was not a fly-fisherman. His rod swung in great arcs, the line thrashing the water violently and tangling hopelessly. After untangling himself from his mess, his next attempt at casting embedded his hook in the wooden gunwale of the rowboat. Quickly losing his patience, our guest hauled in his anchor and came back to the dock, where I met him.

Feeling a bit sheepish, I think, he sagely explained his real reason for renting the boat. He was not there for the fishing. Instead he wanted to take the licence plate numbers of the campers. Then he could trace them for any history of criminal activity that might be related to the gunfire I had heard. I calmly informed him that he could have saved himself a great deal of time and effort just by asking me. I had recorded not only their licence plate numbers, but also their names and addresses when they registered! I gave the officer the information he needed and he quickly departed.

I was less than impressed with the investigative techniques of our "boys in blue" that day. Indirectly, as it happened, the officer's clumsy actions and my advice to him eventually resulted in the mystery being solved.

Later that day another vehicle arrived, interrupting my afternoon chores. It was a blue and white Jimmy bearing the red identification marks of the local Range Patrol. The two middle-aged occupants were very interested in my description of the shot in the night and my cursory investigation the following day. They became especially animated when I told them of the abandoned campsite in the meadow with its curious rectangle of brown grass. They exchanged knowing glances at this point and after sharing a laugh or two at my description of the RCMP fisherman, asked if I could lead them to the spot. Naturally I agreed, wanting to be as helpful as possible.

I told them to follow my truck and was about to leave when the window of the Jimmy rolled down and the driver, with a bit of a grin asked, "Why did you tell the cop not to fish in front of the campsite?"

"Too many people there. You should go by the reeds," I responded eagerly, thinking he might return as a paying customer.

"Why there?" he replied.

"Well, that's where most of the fish are. There's lots of food and shelter for them there."

"Here's a riddle for you," he blared out as his window slowly closed. "If I cast into the reeds to catch fish, why would I camp in a cow pasture?"

I was thoroughly confused by his apparently meaningless

question and started off for the meadow, scratching my head just a little. I screeched to a sudden stop a few minutes later after following the logic in its natural progression. I arrived at the only possible conclusion. Very obviously, if you go to the reeds to catch a fish, then you go to a cow pasture to catch a . . . cow!

The Nicola Plateau is expansive and easily navigated in a four-wheel-drive vehicle. As such, it was easy to access the area without being detected. I learned, much to my surprise, that a number of cattle left to graze the open range from neighbouring ranches had been the targets of a small but active group of rustlers over the past two years.

Stump Lake Ranch, Douglas Lake Cattle Company and the Lauder Ranch had all been victims but the thieves were still at large. They had been able to avoid getting caught because they were efficient and secretive. Their "modus operandi" was unique. As such, their activities were not discovered until days and often weeks after the fact, if at all.

I had often wondered how the ranchers accounted for all their cattle. I had actually thought more than once about how easy it would be to just shoot a nice young steer and throw it in the back of a truck. It seemed so simple. Also, cows died from disease and injury on the open plain. More than once I had come across a bloated carcass in the woods or mired hopelessly in a bog or swamp. Occasionally I found one so weak from illness, that it had to be put down. Whenever this had happened in the past, I had faithfully phoned the ranchers until one day I was told in no uncertain terms that I was wasting their time and I shouldn't bother them anymore!

It seemed impossible with that kind of attitude that they were able to track their losses, regardless of the cause. In fact, they didn't. I discovered later that all ranchers expected to lose a certain percent of the herd. It simply became an accounting line that served as a valuable income tax deduction for the business.

We arrived a short time later at the very same cow pasture that I had taken great pains to clean up the previous day. Proudly I explained how I had cleaned the firepit, gathered all the garbage and assorted refuse and generally tried to return the area to its natural state.

Their disgust and disappointment was evident. They both sneered at me and spit disgusting wads of brown juice onto the ground. The round circles in the back pockets of their jeans revealed the secret of their addiction to Copenhagen, a popular smokeless tobacco. The Range Patrollers explained how I had "done a royal job of screwing things up." In my enthusiasm I had managed to remove or destroy every piece of useful evidence. They had hoped to at least find a clue that would lead them to the identity of the "campers," who were in truth the elusive cattle rustlers.

This location was a recent crime scene; the freshest one the patrollers had yet found. Dark stains on the ground, which I had not even noticed when I was on my cleanup mission or perhaps mistaken for manure, were now abuzz with flies. It was blood!

To my surprise, the two fellows then took shovels from their truck and got busy digging up the rectangular area of dead grass that had puzzled me on the previous visit. They quickly found what they were looking for. One of them let out a loud whoop, dropped his shovel and ran to the truck. Backing up to the pit they had excavated, they took out a chain, connected one end to the towing hook on the vehicle and the other to something partially buried.

As the Jimmy eased forward and the chain became taut, the carcass of a steer gradually materialized from the shallow grave. Once the remains were completely dragged out, I was shocked to see that the entire hind end of the animal was missing. The two rear quarters and the tenderloin area had been removed and the rest just tossed carelessly into the pit. They knocked the red clay off the head of the cow with a spade to reveal the cause of death. A dark, round hole glared obscenely from the animal's forehead. Clearly, it had been shot, the best cuts of meat had been removed and the remains buried to hide the crime.

We re-buried the carcass, seeing no reason to attract bears or other scavengers, and the patrollers left. Somewhat recovered from their initial disappointment and anger at me, they told me to keep a sharp eye out thinking that the rustlers would likely strike again. I was told very clearly to *not* touch another crime scene if I came across one, but call the police immediately instead. As is often the case, I never saw anything out of the ordinary again. About a month later, though, two suspects were arrested and the whole story came out.

The two Merritt men claimed it had all started quite by accident. They both had small farms and regularly supplied beef to friends and neighbours. A few years earlier, they had taken a number of orders but due to an illness in the herd, a number of head of cattle had been lost over the winter. Rather than cancel the orders and send their customers to another supplier, the men had chosen to find another "source" of meat. They made their first visit onto the Nicola Plateau on a moonless night, certain that large ranchers would not miss one or two of their cattle. They seemed to justify their actions by arguing that accidents and sickness likely killed more cows than the one or two they needed to fill their quotas that year. They quickly found it was easier and more profitable to let someone else do the work and pay the expenses. They maintained small, token herds on their home ranches to maintain appearances, but had begun to fill most of their orders with rustled beef instead of home-grown.

The thieves had concocted a simple plan that allowed them to do their dirty work almost undetected. First they would drive into a remote area of the open range and find a small herd of cattle that had bedded down for the night. It was then simple to choose an unfortunate victim or two, quietly approach them in the dark and kill them with a single shot to the head. Then they would erect a large, floorless, canvas tent over the carcasses. One of the men would remove the sod and lay it aside so it could be replaced later. The other would cut away the choice cuts of meat from the animal and pack it in large carrying bags in the back of the truck. The next step was to dig a pit large enough to accommodate what was left of the steer, bury it and pile the excess dirt they removed on top of the bags of meat in the truck. Finally, the sod was replaced, camouflaging any sign of their activity. Then they simply drove away, complete with what appeared to be just a load of dirt. Clearly, the low overhead and sizeable return justified the risk.

Their plan was effective. To make it even more believable, they usually lit a small fire and sometimes set up a clothesline or a couple of deck chairs to create the illusion of a camp. Unfortunately for them, time eventually ran out and the RCMP caught them in the act. In retrospect, though, they should probably consider themselves very lucky. Today's courts just imposed a fine and a suspended sentence. In the past, the normal punishment for cattle rustlers was much more severe. Paying a fine is very civilized and humane when compared to the consequences they might have expected if caught by the ranchers of yesteryear. Traditional justice on the range for cattle rustling would have seen them flogged, bound with barbed wire and dragged behind a horse. Chances of survival in such circumstances were slim.

19

All Good Things

AMONG THE PINES

My soul resides among the pines,
Where up and up and through designs,
Peeks the gem of flawless sky . . .
As if it's hiding; as if it's shy.
The ground beneath is none but moss;
If I should fall, there'd be no loss.
She'd cushion me with open arms,
In all her beauty and all her charm.
Ahead of me and right a ways,
There sits a field of swimming waves.
They stroke the shore with tender care.
How kind this place with me to share.
The sounds about give company
And sing of sheer felicity
They're in my drink and breath and land;
Numerous, just as grains of sand.
So when I write my address down,
With zip code, province, country and town,
My soul reminds me I have lied;
It's among the pines where I reside.

—a tribute to Glimpse Lake by Kari Grain

*A*ll good things, they say, must come to an end. The days between the spring of 1981 and the fall of 1987 passed in the blink of an eye. The lives, goals and aspirations of the eight members of Terra 7 and their families had been changed irrevocably and enhanced unbelievably by our experiences at Glimpse. The success of our venture had been the primary motivation for our activities and the central focus of our lives for seven years, but kids were growing up, parents were aging and priorities were shifting.

The ownership of Glimpse Lake and the re-establishment of a viable business had been the catalyst Kirsti and I needed to escape from the urban insanity. Other things now tapped our time and resources and it was becoming harder and harder to maintain the dedication to our beloved lake. She was simply too greedy and too demanding. There was no room for vacations, soccer camps, birthday parties or socializing outside our narrow group of friends. Something had to change because life was happening and suddenly Glimpse Lake was getting in the way.

Furthermore, our workload had increased astronomically with the opening of the Coquihalla Highway. The new connector eliminated the gruelling seven-hour trek through the Fraser Canyon, which previously was the only route to Glimpse. Suddenly, our season lengthened, the number of clients ballooned, people stayed longer and we began to cater to day guests. The pressure on our facilities, the lake and our energy had become overwhelming.

When the partnership had first been formed, we had agreed to buy the land, try to create a business from a shattered shell and sell the investment within three years, hoping to turn a profit. Almost seven years had passed in the interim. We had been completely inexperienced as first-time business owners. In the beginning, we knew nothing about finances, customer service or the outdoors. None of us were mechanics, carpenters, roofers or loggers. We didn't know a toadstool from a skunk cabbage, but in spite of the obstacles, we had performed a minor miracle. Utilizing creativity, research and simple hard work, we had re-established a respectable, profitable business. For all intents and purposes, we had achieved what we set out to do.

Our accomplishments were huge. The annual income had ballooned from less than ten thousand to over fifty thousand dollars. The cabins and lodge had been renovated and updated with new appliances. The old boats had been replaced. We installed hot water, flush toilets, laundry facilities, showers and a septic system. The wiring had been renewed in all the buildings and commercial power brought in from almost ten miles away, eliminating the need for the generator. We logged some of the mature timber, creating an expanded camping area as well as generating a much-needed injection of cash. In the process, each of us had grown or matured in a different way, but it was time to move on.

We never anticipated having the experience turn into a labour of love and we were now faced with a dilemma. The business had to be sold yet many of us were attached to the land with a passion that could not be reconciled. Even our children begged us not to sell, not understanding that it was largely their wants and needs that created the crisis. No amount of money would ease the pain of the loss we knew would accompany the pending sale.

Kirsti and I had agreed with Jack and Jennifer, the only other partners who had small children, that when it came time to sell, we wanted to keep at least a small piece of land for the kids. Hoping the day would never arrive, we had never seriously considered the options that we had.

The time had come to do so, and we began looking into the possibility of subdividing the acreage into two sections; the larger one to be sold with the business and a smaller one to be shared by any partners who wanted to participate. We had hoped that the money we received from the sale of the larger piece would be enough to pay off the mortgage, leaving us with a free title on the remaining lot. Not only would it be paid for, it would be a place we could come anytime and something we could pass on.

So, we took our idea to the Land Title Office in Kamloops, where we met with the appropriate people. From the outset, they were officious and uncooperative. They were immediately opposed to our proposal and advised us to abandon the idea.

"No," they said. "It can't be done." Because of the twenty-four waterfront lots and the second and third tier lots created in the initial subdivision in the late sixties, the lake was considered to be "fully developed." By definition, this designation prevented any further development of buildings or other lots on the lake, thus preventing us from subdividing our 160 acres into two sections. We were also told that even if any subdivision was permitted, which it was not, there would be caveats. We would be responsible for dedicating a public access every few hundred metres and even signing over a deed to the Province of BC for the road. We would have to widen it, provide adequate ditching and culverts as well as other unspecified "services." Understandably, this would involve us incurring certain additional costs. Already the government was claiming ownership of the road, arguing that someone had requested the road be ploughed at some unspecified time in the recent past. The red tape was unbelievable but typical of government bureaucracy.

Our idea of subdividing the property into two sections was quickly quashed so we created a new plan. If we were not allowed to subdivide, maybe we could use the strata title regulations to divide the property into shares and sell some or all of them. The idea of strata title was relatively new and had been used extensively and successfully in apartments and condos but never to our knowledge with resort properties.

It was really quite simple. First, we could lease the business to be run at arm's length by a third party, thus removing the time commitment and workload. Second, we could divide the remaining property into a number of waterfront lots, which could then be sold on a strata basis or leased on a long-term basis to interested parties. Each partner could retain a section of his or her choice and the rest would be sold or leased, insuring a steady and reliable cash flow. I was tremendously excited! It was an excellent long-term plan, and as hindsight would prove, the path we really should have taken.

In the years since the lodge was sold, recreational property has been in great demand. There are now many properties in the southern part of the province that are time-shared, stratified and utilized in other creative fashions to maximize their business potential. With the steadily increasing real estate values, the influx of foreign investors, the devalued dollar and the commercial emphasis on outdoor leisure-time activities, a holding of land in the wilderness is a much-sought-after luxury. The value of the Glimpse Lake land currently is in the millions.

The strata/lease plan would have worked, for we had many parties interested in making the investment. Unfortunately the plan did not suit the needs of all the partners. Some had no interest in being involved any longer in the lake and wanted to find a solution that would see their investment returned in the shortest time possible. Our only alternative was for the remaining partners to buy out those who wanted to leave and then try to implement the strata title strategy with those who were left. This was beyond our budget and therefore impossible, so the decision was made to list the property for sale with a real estate broker. By the fall of 1987 it had not sold, and some of our group had become very discouraged.

The partners were simply not prepared to invest more money and another year of labour in the lodge. Our annual general meeting on the Thanksgiving weekend that year was not our happiest. It was truly a camp divided. Some were concerned about not having sold yet; others about having to sell at all.

Many investors had expressed interest and we had actually considered some offers. Each party, however, was forced to withdraw their offer after being unable to obtain financing from their banks. There was not a big market for fishing camps in the late eighties, perhaps because the banking institutions still viewed the financing of such ventures with scepticism and scorn. They saw little value or security in 160 acres of isolated forest with almost one mile of lake frontage in the high country of the Nicola Plateau of BC. They felt that a business with such a short season was a bad risk, in spite of our efforts to convince them of the untapped potential. We argued without luck that Glimpse Lake Lodge could expand its scope to take advantage of the growing interest in other outdoor and winter activities.

European banks had no such misgivings or qualms, though. In fact, as we would discover, they were actively seeking sound real estate investments in Canada, especially southern BC. Consequently, it was the narrow vision of the Canadian lending institutions and their unwillingness to support local entrepreneurs that ultimately resulted in foreign investors being the benefactors in this saga.

I had organized the Terra 7 group initially so many years ago and arranged for the purchase of the property. Somehow I felt an obligation to get us all out now that things had changed. I had been watching classified sections regularly and first saw the advertisement in the *Vancouver Sun* in the "Property Wanted" section. Someone wanted a wilderness retreat in southern BC. It had to be deeded land on a small lake at least a quarter section in area and isolated from its neighbours. It sounded very much like they were describing Glimpse Lake! Included was a post box number that an interested party could sent details to. After getting the okay from my partners, I put together a presentation including a description of the property, a list of assets, an income statement and some photographs. I casually dropped it in the mail a few days later, expecting that to be the end. How wrong I was.

Within days an agent representing an interested party in Switzerland contacted me. It seemed that Glimpse Lake Lodge was exactly what his clients wanted and I was asked to provide more information. I contacted the potential buyer by telephone, and after a short discussion, they asked if I could show them the property. I explained that because it was late October the business was closed for the winter and it was already very cold in the high country. Viewing the property in the spring, I explained, would give them a much better perspective of the business and the lay of the land. However, they insisted on taking a look as soon as possible, which surprised me even more considering they would be flying in from Europe by the end of the week to take the tour!

On the appointed date, with very mixed feelings, I fetched two gentlemen from the Kelowna airport and drove the three hours to the camp. It was a quiet journey; one of the longest I had every made. I realized that to justify a trip from Europe just to look at a piece of property, these potential buyers must be very serious indeed. Arriving at the lake, my guests asked to be given some time to wander around and walk the property lines alone. I thought that was a strange request as I believed I was there to provide explanations and to answer their questions. With a sudden shock, I realized that I was about to lose my lake; my dream was evaporating like the morning mist; a loss for which I had not prepared myself.

The drive back to Kelowna is a memory that shall remain with me forever. They wanted the property and were prepared to pay the full asking price provided we could complete the deal within two weeks. There were no financing arrangements to be made as they had the investment capital waiting to be spent. Reluctantly, pending the approval of the partners, I accepted the offer and by the end of November 1987, Glimpse Lake Lodge was sold and ceased to exist as a fishing camp.

Our family made its final trip to Glimpse Lake Lodge on the last weekend of October to say goodbye and gather a remembrance or two of our experience. Appropriately we stayed in Cabin 17, the one we rented when we first came to Glimpse over two decades before. Our boys were nine and twelve and our daughter only four. Already, our sons were anticipating the coming ski season and would have been just as happy to be back in Kelowna for the annual ski swap. Like the boys before her, our daughter Kari was discovering the wonders of nature at Glimpse Lake and constantly peppered us with questions. Where do the frogs go in the winter? Who will feed the mice when we are gone? Why do fish eat worms? Do brown cows give brown milk?

It was a gorgeous fall weekend with clear, warm days and crisp, frosty nights. The air was fresh and revitalizing and a paper-thin skiff of ice tinkled melodiously in the rustling stalks of bulrushes. Reeds rimmed the shore and glistened with the same golden hue as the larch needles and aspen leaves. Squirrels chattered noisily, anxious to put in their last caches before the grip of winter once again brought the world to a frozen standstill. The aromatic woodsmoke curled lazily from the chimney of the lodge and settled like a blanket over the back meadow, creating an almost ethereal atmosphere.

Hand in hand, Kirsti and I took a last walk through the tall grass in the fields. The kids screamed with joy as they ran down the path, playing tag and teasing each other. My daughter, in the simple way that only a child can, put it all together very clearly.

"Since you don't have to work all day, can you take me fishing?" she said to us innocently. "Yes," I mused. "There are other priorities."

I realized this chapter had concluded in our book of life, but I was buoyed by the knowledge that there were many more adventures ahead of us. This was only the first port in a voyage that we had begun as starry-eyed newlyweds full of optimism and naïveté. The journey was far from over!

It took me a long time to achieve final closure and understand the true value in the adventure of owning Glimpse Lake Lodge. For many years I harboured remorse and regret, feeling I had lost my dream. However, with the maturity that age brings, I finally realized that in fact, we truly had achieved our dreams and our goals. We had left the city behind for good, and with our children had become "country" folk, experienced outdoorsmen. We had taken our place and become a part of the long and honourable history of the Nicola Plateau started so many years ago by courageous pioneers like Bob and Helen Albrecht. As a matter of course, the new owners would also become part of that history. I came to appreciate that the real reward in our experience of Glimpse Lake was not in the ownership, as I had long assumed, but in the wealth of memories, the rich experiences and the lessons in life that they taught. They can never be taken away and I can visit them anytime, for my heart, too, resides among the pines at Glimpse Lake.

Epilogue

irsti and I still return to Glimpse Lake, usually two or three times a year, to enjoy the fishing and the memories. Almost always, we come across someone with whom we are able to recollect with fondness the old days at Glimpse. They were magical and I wouldn't trade them for anything. Even now, I chuckle or shed a tear at those wondrous events.

Of the original eight partners who bought Glimpse Lake Lodge in 1981, six still live in the Lower Mainland area. My father passed away in 1999 and my mother in 2006. Kirsti and I still live in Kelowna. Our son John-Erik and his wife Tracey, after their marriage in June 2003, spent their honeymoon camped at Glimpse, somehow completing the circle. I was never able to find Bob Albrecht and at the time of writing, Ted Grant, now in his eighties, still visits the lake to go fishing occasionally.

Today the old Glimpse Lake Lodge property is still owned by the 1987 buyers and is known as "Little Beaver Creek Ranch." It can be accessed at www.littlebeavercreekranch.com. It has a huge popularity with European customers and has been well marketed overseas. It provides many amenities, most of which we could only dream so many years ago. Guests can enjoy horseback riding and bicycling in the summer as well as ice skating or sleigh rides in the winter. Some Saturday nights they even fire up the barbecues to cook steaks and hamburgers, followed by dancing on the veranda to live country music!

However, it has little if any resemblance to the old camp. In the first few years after the sale, millions of dollars were invested. The entire 160 acres was fenced and a massive gate was erected at the entranceway. The old road that once passed through the campground along the shore of the lake was moved up the hill. The shell of the old lodge remains but the inside has been totally modernized with oak, wainscoting, elaborate wallpaper and opulent furniture. An antique bar that once graced the inside of a Caribou-Chilcotin hotel greets guests as they enter. Most of the cabins were demolished, making room for three beautiful log homes and a large horse stable. A sprawling structure reminiscent of a luxury spa or hotel has been erected on the flat, sandy point just past the main entrance.

I wish to thank the Merritt Museum for their assistance, Joe Lauder for his historical perspective on the Glimpse Lake area, James Procter for his invaluable information on George Procter, my wonderfully creative daughter Kari for the use of her poem, "Among the Pines," my partners in Terra 7 Investments and Ronda Barzilay & Associates. Also, I wish to thank my family, who endured my passion, idiosyncrasies and foibles with understanding and love. Most of all, I wish to thank my wife, Kirsti. She is a most remarkable woman, for she is able to share me without harbouring any jealousy or resentment. From her understanding, I draw strength, confidence and the freedom to luxuriate in Nature's masterpiece. Fortunate indeed I am, to be wakened at dawn on a frosty fall morning with the suggestive whisper, "John, wake up. I hear your lake calling you."

Appendix

Fishing Glimpse Lake

Since Bob Albrecht first stocked Glimpse Lake so many years ago, it is the fishing that has drawn visitors to this scenic lake. There are many factors that combine to make Glimpse a unique and productive fishery. It has an outflow which is dammed and controlled for irrigation purposes. It also has an inflow stream which, when properly maintained, provides a fertile spawning bed for rainbow trout. The lush vegetation on the lake bottom and around the shore provides protection and a natural habitat for insects. The abundant food supply causes the fish to grow very quickly. The lake itself is very deep in places, providing a sanctuary for the fish during the heat of summer or when the fishing pressure is great.

The depth of the lake also helps ensure there is good circulation and plenty of oxygen available during the winter freeze-up. This minimizes the chance of winterkill. Winterkills can occur when the ice, which forms on the lake in November, gets covered with a thick layer of snow, blocking the light of the sun during the short winter days. The lack of sunlight prevents the process of photosynthesis in the underwater plant life and therefore the production of oxygen. In shallow lakes, the oxygen in the water can become depleted more quickly and the fish can die from asphyxiation. This is a common phenomenon during long, cold winters and has the potential to kill the entire fish population, making the lake completely barren.

The "human" factor also contributes greatly to the viability of the fishery in Glimpse. Regular stocking of the lake by the Ministry of Wildlife, an ice-fishing ban during the winter and building restrictions on the lakeshore are steps that have enhanced the lake's productivity. Fishermen help their own cause by employing catch-and-release fishing practices and adhering to the electric motor-only policy. Barring unanticipated pressures or disasters, the prospects for the future of Glimpse Lake are very positive.

Winter departs very reluctantly on the Nicola Plateau. Because of the elevation, it is often late April before the snow starts to melt. In fact, the ice has been known to remain on the lake well into May, relinquishing its greedy grip only at the insistence of the lengthening days and unpredictable winds that race across its surface. Once the breakup starts, it is only a matter of days amidst grunts, groans and haunting howls, that the cracks widen and the lake is once again free of ice. Spring has arrived.

The pussywillows pop and the buds on the spindly aspens strain impatiently at their husks in an explosion of life. Birds seem to appear from nowhere and the only thing louder than their mating calls is the moaning of the relentless wind in the evergreens lining the shore. Freshets and rivulets, final remnants of the howling blizzards of winter, tumble over the rocks, quenching the thirst of the lake and filling her ample girth to overflow. Mice and chipmunks scurry timidly searching for tidbits. Black bears and ferrets are more bold and are almost frantic after waking from months of hibernation. Their rumbling stomachs remind them of voracious appetites that must be satisfied.

Spring too is the time when a silent and invisible miracle takes place beneath the surface of the lake. Soon after the ice leaves, close inspection would reveal the existence of the larvae of a small midge-type fly apparently just floating under the surface. These creatures, called chironomids by fly-fishermen, are often less than one-quarter of an inch in length. They are among the earliest to awaken and have actually hatched from eggs in the muddy bottom. They drift to the surface lazily in thick masses. They occur in such abundance that a hungry trout will merely swim through a cloud of them with its mouth open, rather than dine on individual insects. The challenge for the fisherman is to imitate the colour and size of the hatching insect. Only then can he present the fly in the location of a hatch and sink the hook before the lazy trout, recognizing an imitation, spits out the offering in favour of the real thing. Using the chironomid, which forms a substantial portion of the diet of a Kamloops trout in the spring, a fisherman will often be rewarded with a very memorable experience or, if unable to "match the hatch," will be skunked.

In the larvae form, survivors of the journey to the surface will hatch, struggling from the gluey surface tension in an attempt to achieve their sole ambition: reproduction. This may occur in a matter of hours and in short order, the lake will be strewn with empty casings and the bodies of millions of these tiny flies. Strangely, though the larvae appear to be a delicacy for the hungry fish, the terrestrial, the airborne fly, is seldom targeted for a meal.

Another very obvious form of aquatic life is the freshwater shrimp or scud, which is not really an insect, but rather a crustacean. Glimpse has a wide variety of shrimp ranging in size from microscopic to almost a full inch in length. The colour can vary from bluish to green, yellow or orange. However, the illusion of an orange shrimp scampering along the bottom or in the weeds is usually created by the coloration of a small mass of orange eggs found on the underbelly of the female during the spring. Many fishermen routinely take samples of the contents of a trout's stomach before releasing it or after it has been gutted. A Glimpse Lake trout will always reveal shrimp of some kind, reinforcing the long-held opinion of many that the most reliable fly in the box may not imitate an insect at all but actually a shrimp.

Glimpse abounds in an interesting array of leeches, which also supplement the diet of resident trout. Although usually black, it is common to find leeches mottled with red or brown and reaching up to four inches or more in length when fully elongated. They are generally found near the shore, under rocks and near the bottom. Although most famous for their blood-sucking ability, it is rare to see a leech attached to a swimmer. A leech pattern fly, anything long, undulating and dark, can be fished very effectively at times. Unlike a strike on a chironomid, trout will attack a leech aggressively, so it can be very successful if trolled slowly.

In spite of the stories and legends surrounding the leech, the most fearsome denizen of the freshwater deep by far, is the dragonfly nymph. Before the iridescent dragonfly hatches and takes to the air, it too must endure childhood and adolescence in the larval form. Unlike the helicopter-like terrestrial, the nymph looks and behaves like a monster! Sometimes up to three inches in length, it can be found lurking in the weeds searching for an unsuspecting quarry, which when found, it attacks with a viciousness seldom seen. With twin razor-like mandibles, the dragonfly nymph will clamp, vice-like, onto anything from a careless shrimp to a fisherman's finger. I have been told that a large dragonfly nymph can break a match stick with its jaws, though I have never tried to prove it.

One of the relics I retrieved from the jumbled mess in the stairwell of the old lodge was a poem, signed with just the single name "Barbara" and dated 12/23/66. Probably written to be sung to the English tune "Sing a Song of Sixpence," it seems to define the fishing at Glimpse Lake.

SING A SONG OF GLIMPSE LAKE

Sing a song of Glimpse Lake
A pocket full of flies
Four and twenty flatfish
Will surely bring a rise.
When the smokehouse opens
George begins to sing,
"Isn't that a dainty dish
Fit for any king?"
The dogs are in a meadow
Routing out a quail
While Sue weeps o'er a Kamloops
That hasn't any tail
Wil is up a Story's End
Doing mighty fine
When along comes an osprey

And snips off his line!
Ray has hooked a lunker
He knows the prize will take
But the fish leaps out the trusty net
And swims away uplake.
Barbara's on the near bank
Basking in the sun
When along comes a black bear
And puts her on the run!
Bob is in the pumphouse
Wrestling with some gear
And Helen stalks a mushroom
In a woodland spot quite near.
With Solunar Table guidance,
We fish the fading light
And listen as the loons cry
And call out in the night.
The Milky Way beguiles us,
The cattle trail away
And we hurry off to Cabin F
To plot another day.

The two main methods of fishing Glimpse are fly-fishing and trolling with a hook and worm. Both techniques can be highly productive. Sometimes, though, success is determined just by the mood of the lake.

One of the biggest fish I saw come out of the lake, a five-pound trophy, was taken in the middle of a hot, calm day by a woman who was just a beginner. She was fishing from shore, a rare event on Glimpse. There had been a prolonged hot spell and a prolific ant hatch the day before. The fish were lethargic and lazy, having feasted on the abundant insect life. Few fish, if any, were being taken even by the most experienced fisherman. The odds were stacked against her!

From a rusty old tackle box, the lady pulled out a large, gaudy spoon with two sets of large treble hooks hanging threateningly from its underbelly. With a series of unknown knots, she tied it to her line.

She told me later that the lure was something her father had used many summers before to catch northern pike in Saskatchewan. On her first attempt to launch the offensive piece of metal into the lake, her back-cast caught firmly on a small aspen tree. Her line broke cleanly and forced her to climb the sapling to get the lure back. Her next attempt was similarly disappointing as the hook splashed unceremoniously into the water and buried itself into the mud at her feet. Finally on her third try, the lady coordinated all the motions and the lure arched into the lake gracefully, and splashed noisily in the middle of the tangled reeds. I smirked knowingly, as her rod bent double and the reel screamed. I was certain she had become snagged and was curious as to how she would handle her predicament.

A large splash, a few metres out in the clear water and well away from the reeds, suddenly caught my attention and I stared in awe as the line from the lady's rod cut smoothly through the surface. She had a fish, a big one, and it was heading for open water! Her screams of delight brought old and young alike from all around to watch the unlikely event. Luckily for her, the line was strong and it held as she horsed the doomed fish to shore. There it flopped obscenely, until finally she grabbed it firmly by the tail and beat it senseless on a handy rock. Proudly, blood streaming down her arms, she held up the five-pound monster to the cheers, smiles and shaking heads of the surprised onlookers. Within moments, she had it gutted and filleted, and ready for the night's feast! Sometimes lady luck can be the best lure in the tackle box!

Most people, though, fish Glimpse Lake from a boat or float-tube. Trollers most often use a spin casting rod or bait casting rod with some kind of "hardware" attached to the end. The hook itself is usually a barbed Number 4 or 6 bait hook with a large, wriggling gob of earthworms impaled upon it. Directly above the bait is a series of swivelling, gyrating spinners that twirl as the line passes through the water. Finally, a weight or sinker is used to take the line deeper. The "Ford Fender" or "Willow Leaf" as it is often called, is then trolled behind the boat and attracts the fish, which then eat the bait. This method is often the surest way of catching something and is especially popular for beginners. Sometimes, instead of using live bait, the hook and worm will be replaced with a small spoon or spinner to attract the fish. A common alternative is a "Flatfish," which comes in varying colours, a "Dick Nite" or a "Spin'n Glo."

Some fly-fishermen would argue that trolling is less sporting than fly-fishing because when trolling, it is often hard to tell if there is a fish on the line. The weight of the gear and the action of the lure going through the water is similar to a small, fighting fish. Consequently, it is common for a troller to catch a fish and not even know it, mistaking the fighting of the fish for the movement of the lure. Also, the chances of a released fish surviving after being horsed in by a troller are much less than those for a released fish after being caught on a short fly line with a barbless hook.

Fly-fishing is a sport that has grown geometrically in popularity in recent years and is by far the most popular method on Glimpse. It can be done by drifting a fly, trolling it or casting it. In all cases, the equipment used has basic similarities, but when casting a fly, the equipment must be "matched." This means the weight of the rod and the weight of the line must be similar. For example a five-weight rod must be used to properly cast a five-weight line. If a four- or a six-weight line is used with a five-weight rod, it will still work, but the fisherman may not be able to cast as far or as smoothly and still present the fly naturally.

Most fly-fishing on the interior lakes of BC is done with a five- to seven-weight rod between eight-and-a-half and ten feet long. The most common rod materials are fibreglass, bamboo, graphite and boron and can cost from less than fifty dollars to well over a thousand! Rod, reel and line combinations can be bought relatively cheaply from big box stores, but the quality is generally questionable at best. Even a beginning fly-fisherman should buy good quality equipment for the best fly-fishing experience. An avid fly-fisherman will usually own three or four rods of varying weights. Orvis, Fenwick, Sage and Loomis, among many others, make fine rods for every level and can be bought for less than a few hundred dollars. Many fly-fishermen have their rods custom-made to match their particular styles and preferences. Custom-made rods start around three hundred dollars and go up.

A fly reel is probably the least important component of the package. In reality, a fly reel is usually only used as a place to store the line. It is also used for the odd occasion when more line than the flyline itself is required to play a fish and land it successfully. Sometimes a large fish will take a run, stripping all the flyline from the reel. Without emergency line on the reel, a fisherman could run out, snapping off the fish when it reached the end. Therefore, the first thing on any fly reel is about fifty metres of strong, braided Dacron line, called backing. The flyline is then attached to the backing to provide the extra length when needed.

The flyline is probably the most important part of a fly-fishing combination because the line takes the fly to the correct depth. It also allows the fisherman to present the fly in the most natural way; that which most closely imitates the movement of the natural insect. The line itself averages ninety feet in length, has a braided fibre core and is surrounded with a plastic coating. The core provides the stretch, stiffness and strength of the line while the coating enhances the performance and provides colour.

Flylines vary by weight, density and shape. Different line weights match the rods and allow the fisherman to "load" the rod and cast the line. Different densities permit the line to float or sink. Different shapes or tapers are designed to concentrate the weight of the line in certain locations, depending upon the need of the fisherman to cast longer distances or achieve delicate presentations. Every fly-fisherman should buy good quality lines. Products made by Scientific Angler, Cortland, Mastery, Sage and Rio continue to supply much of the market and can usually be purchased for under seventy-five dollars. Because they are so expensive, anglers should make sure they clean their lines frequently, prevent exposure to insect repellents and keep them out of direct sunlight whenever possible. A flyline will last a long time if it is looked after properly.

A floating line, as it suggests, floats for its entire length, allowing the angler to present a fly on the surface without having it sink. When fish are feeding on the surface, taking the terrestrial form of insects like mayflies or caddis flies, a floating line is the main tool and has the advantage of being able to be used in very shallow water without snagging.

As trout generally feed on the surface for only about ten percent of the time, a floating or dry line may not be as important as a sinking or wet line. A sinking line is constructed to sink for its entire length, and is used to take the fly to the depth that fish are feeding most actively. Often, this is near the bottom as trout enjoy leeches, freshwater shrimp and the larvae and pupae of the dragonfly, damselfly or caddis fly. Because of this, a sinking line is the most important line in a fly-fisherman's box.

Most aquatic insects hatch from the mud, swim to the surface and emerge as terrestrials to become airborne, mate and die. As such, much of their brief life is spent on the voyage to the surface of the pond or lake. At this time, they are easy prey for fish, so a fly-fisherman often needs to present his fly at various depths to enjoy success. This may require a third type of flyline, a sinking tip. Again, as it suggests, only the tip, the first fifteen to thirty feet of the flyline actually sinks, while the remainder floats on the surface. This allows the fisherman to fish the intermediate zone between the bottom and the surface of the lake.

Because it is difficult and time-consuming to physically replace lines when needed, fly-fishermen often have their lines on separate reels or spools that can be quickly switched to meet changing conditions. To prevent changes in lines at all, some fishermen may actually carry three different rods, each with a different type of line attached.

Everyone has a secret fly, technique or spot for fishing Glimpse Lake and most fly-fishermen are anxious to share their successes. In truth, they are quite a generous lot and if some interest is shown, they are often willing to pass on a sample of their favourite fly. This is the way I have collected many of the proven patterns that have given our family hours of enjoyment.

I have also lost my share of flies. When casting a fly and slowly retrieving it to the boat, a fish will often strike very hard. In the case of a large fish, he will often either rip the hook out of its mouth, snap off the fly or even straighten the hook if the line is held too tightly. It takes a great deal of concentration and self-control to let a fish run when it hits rather than jerk the line and "set" the hook. Even a small trout can hit a fly with amazing force and easily break a three- or four-pound test leader. Therefore, it is not usually necessary to pull back on the line when a fish strikes.

Carelessness can empty a fly box in short order. It can also be very expensive, as I once discovered while trying to manoeuvre my boat in a strong wind. Casting had not been productive and the wind had become too strong to cast easily. After my anchor had broken free for the second time, I decided to troll my fly instead.

Operating a boat, especially one made of aluminum in a Glimpse Lake wind, can be really challenging. Trying to troll a fly at the same time can be positively frustrating because both hands are needed for the oars. As a result, I arranged a system whereby I could lean the rod out one side of the boat and tuck the handle under my knee. When a fish hit I would just grab the rod and play the fish, hopefully before the wind blew me into the reeds. This had worked very well until one day I hit an especially large fish.

I was rowing into the teeth of a strong afternoon wind and had turned a corner into a narrows where two reed beds almost meet. The caddis flies were hatching and on the foamy surface, large trout could be seen rolling all around me, feasting on the plump insects. In a heartbeat, my rod-tip doubled. It was followed by a single scream from the ratchet on the fly reel, which stopped unexpectedly. Then the rod was torn from where it had lain cradled behind my legs. It was a combination of setting the drag too tightly and simply not hanging on well enough. Letting go of the oars, I made a desperate, unsuccessful lunge for the rod. In a commotion and clatter that only a fly reel can make as it smashes and bounces on the bottom of an aluminum boat, my precious Fenwick rod disappeared over the back of the boat! I looked up to see a gorgeous trout, with my fly firmly attached to the side of its mouth, leap a couple of feet out of the water as if mocking me, and disappear. Cursing my stupidity, I dredged the lake unsuccessfully for two days with a home-made grappling hook hoping to snag my rod. I did, though, land a spin casting outfit complete with a Canadian Tire price tag of $29.95! A poor trade, I thought, and a costly lesson.

Dry fly-fishing is supposed to be much more relaxing than that.

On a warm day or evening when the fish are visibly rising, a properly presented dry or floating fly tied on a Number 12 or smaller hook can be very rewarding. The fly should be presented gently on a dry line as close as possible to the reeds and if breezy, on the lee side. Once on the water, the fly should be left to sit for a few moments before being twitched gently, and then slowly retrieved. The fish will usually hit very hard and the most difficult thing is to avoid jerking the rod tip. I long ago discovered that the best way to guard against this is to hold the rod parallel to the surface of the lake as soon as the cast is completed. "Retrieve the line, don't lift the rod," is a good rule of thumb.

At times, it might look like the fish are taking caddis flies or damselflies off the surface, yet after many casts, a fisherman gets no bites. When this happens, the fish are often taking the insects in the top twelve inches of water, before they emerge from their casings to hatch. Often, trying a larger hook, a Number 8 or 10 extra long, dressed as a half-back or 52 Buick and a sinking tip line will be the answer. The first cast or two will likely tell the story. I have even used the small Muddler Minnow, dragged just below the surface on a sinking tip with great success.

When the lake seems quiet and there are neither fish nor birds active, the trout can be and often are still feeding deeper down. This is the time to use a full sinking line. Often, a lot of patience and trial and error is needed until the right pattern is found. Until the first fish is in the boat and its stomach contents checked, it might be impossible to determine what the fish are eating that day. Therefore I usually start by trying a Number 8 or 10 nymph such as a black Doc Sprately, full-back or dragonfly pattern. If that doesn't work, the next step might be a green shrimp, black leech or red blood leech. Fished with a very slow retrieve, close to the bottom, one of these patterns is almost guaranteed to give a thrill or two.

Just as the journey, not the destination is often the best part of the trip, even the best fisherman will occasionally be skunked on Glimpse. For the past four decades I have fished this lake. Every year I find that the feeding habits of the fish are slightly different, requiring a modification to the fly pattern or presentation. Sometimes every effort fails and I return to camp having enjoyed nothing more than the songs of the birds, the touch of the sun, the breeze on my face and the intoxicating perfume of the pines. And that is more than enough.